NINETEENTH-CENTURY HISTORIANS
OF NEW HAVEN

Drawn & Engraved by J.W.Barber

E VIEW OF THE PUBLIC SQUARE OR GREEN IN NEW HAVEN CON.
On the left, Trinity Ch.(Episcopal); on the right, North Ch. between are Center Church & State House; near Trinity Ch., in the distance is seen (a) Townsend block on the site of Pres.Clap's house. — The graves of Gov. Eaton and the Regicides are back of Center Ch.

New Haven Green circa 1855. Drawn and engraved by J. W. Barber

Nineteenth-Century Historians of New Haven

by
Richard Hegel

ARCHON BOOKS 1972

Library of Congress Cataloging in Publication Data

Hegel, Richard, 1927-
Nineteenth-century historians of New Haven.

Bibliography: p.
1. New Haven—Historiography. I. Title.
F104.N6H43   974.6'7'072024   70-181318
ISBN 0-208-01262-1

Printed in the United States of America

To Linda

Contents

Illustrations

Preface

The purpose of this survey is to define the contributions to New Haven historiography of Leonard Bacon, John Warner Barber, Edward R. Lambert, Edward E. Atwater and Charles H. Levermore, the only New Haven historical writers of significance in the nineteenth century. To provide a background, the general trends of American historical writing during the nineteenth century have been traced. Several works of both Bacon and Barber, the most prolific of the group, were chosen as representative of their writings, in addition to the important historical works on New Haven of the other three. These writings are reviewed with special emphasis on the use of source material, style of presentation, methodology, viewpoint, and completeness.

The works chosen are as follows:

Bacon, Leonard. *Thirteen Historical Discourses, on the Completion of Two Hundred Years, from the Beginning of The First Church in New Haven.* (1839).

Bacon, Leonard, *Slavery Discussed in Occasional Essays from 1833 to 1846.* (1846).

Bacon, Leonard. "Civil Government in The New Haven Colony," *Papers of The New Haven Colony Historical Society.* Vol. I. (1865) Pp. 11-27.

Barber, John Warner. *History and Antiquities of New Haven, (Conn.) from its Earliest Settlement to the Present Time.* (1831).

Barber, John Warner. *Connecticut Historical Collections.* Second edition. (1836).

Barber, John W. (comp.) *A History of the Amistad Captives.* (1840).

Lambert, Edward R. *History of The Colony of New Haven, Before and After the Union with Connecticut.* (1838).

Atwater, Edward E. *History of The Colony of New Haven to its Absorption into Connecticut.* (1881).

Atwater, Edward E. (ed.). *History of The City of New Haven.* (1887).

Levermore, Charles H. *The Republic of New Haven: A History of Municipal Evolution.* (1886).

The sequence of my work follows this same order. A biographical sketch introduces each chapter dealing with an individual author.

Richard Hegel

New Haven
Connecticut
1971

A Survey of the General Field of Nineteenth-Century American Historiography

with particular attention to local historical writing and the influence of local historical societies

The study of American historiography is a rapidly expanding field, and an examination of historical writing and compilation is one of history's most interesting aspects. The fact that many historians have overlooked the literary phase of their work should also lead to an examination of methods of historical presentation. The founding of the Library of Congress in 1800 facilitated the preservation of historical materials on which studies could be based. During this period it was realized that major portions of American colonial and revolutionary history were recorded in British as well as in other European government archives.[1] A considerable number of local histories prepared during the early years of the United States were motivated by national pride and interpreted local events from a national viewpoint. This approach waned in time as people showed a greater interest in local history as such.

Many early nineteenth-century historians discovered that obtaining publication was a formidable task. This was often the case with New Haven's John Warner Barber, and he frequently became his own publisher. There was a rapid growth of local historiography after 1815 partially as a reaction to the expansion of nationalism and also as a reflection of the competition between different areas of the country. Local antiquarians wished to safeguard the history and reputation of their own areas as well as to see that it would not be overlooked. To secure for his own locality its rightful place in history and its due recognition the local historiographer often wrote the history of his own region himself, coupling it with national events stressing local importance and differentiating his own from other areas. John Warner Barber's *History and Antiquities of New Haven* as well as his *Connecticut Historical Collections* are examples of this type of writing.

In the first part of the nineteenth century a reverence for ancestors was an important theme in historical writing. Competition existed between local historiographers in the production of works elevating the virtues of the forefathers. Such an overtone is clearly evident in Edward R. Lambert's *History of The Colony of New Haven*, and Leonard Bacon's *Thirteen Historical Discourses*, which also deals with early New Haven. During the period after the War of 1812 there developed a wish to have the United States obtain an "American character." It was urged that American history be given greater emphasis in the schools. To supply materials many authors prepared textbooks. The enactment of state laws requiring school instruction in American history further stimulated the production of American historiography. Many of these textbooks were written by New Englanders. Such works highlighted New England's role and they were used throughout the country. A majority of them selected as their authority Abiel Holmes' *American Annals.*[2] Holmes (the son-in-law of Ezra Stiles, president of Yale) sought to comprehend American history in its totality and hoped that his book would be more than a chronology, although essentially it was only slightly better.[3]

During the first half of the nineteenth century the majority of American historical writers generally did not use original source material.[4] John Warner Barber acknowledges his dependency on Holmes' *American Annals* in the preface to his *Interesting Events in the History of the United States*.[5] In the early 1800s documentary histories such as Barber's *History and Antiquities of New Haven* and also his *Connecticut Historical Collections* were popular. The latter includes the names of the early Connecticut settlers and founders as well as many accounts of various localities within the state. Barber's *Interesting Events in the History of the United States* is also representative of this type of history.[6] The greater number of American historical writers after the Revolution and during the first half of the nineteenth century understood the purpose of their writings to be expression of the ideals of a new and vigorous country.[7]

Jared Sparks, who at one time was president of Harvard, is noted for conserving documents and also for his efforts in behalf of telling the story of the War of Independence. At one time during the 1820s he was owner of the *North American Review* which exercised a powerful influence over the fortunes of new books. He is credited with beginning for American historians the practice of going to Europe for sources of American history. While Sparks' name is connected with a large body of historical works, a great portion of his writings are of an editorial nature. Studies centering about the American Revolution were quite popular during the first half of the nineteenth century. These writings may best be illustrated by George Bancroft's narrative *History of the United States*. He was essentially preoccupied with the Revolution and is noted for his attempt to raise events from their local setting to give them international significance. Bancroft's work rapidly became the standard American history, and it has been stated that he brought order out of the records of America's past.[8] He obtained source material from foreign archives—writers of such narrative histories as his were in effect publishers of source materials.[9] George Bancroft was truly the first national historian and his historical writings were well adapted to the public need. American historians had not yet begun to write mainly for each other.[10] Statements of a belief in progress, well-suited to the American character, can often be found in the works of nineteenth-century historical writers. At times they are scattered throughout the narrative, as in the histories of Bancroft, or often stated in a preface.[11]

During the middle of the century the school of romantic nationalism became prominent. Writers influenced by romantic nationalism believed they had a mission to disseminate the story of the progress of freedom, with their message being incorporated in the history of the United States. While each writer possessed his own concept of the nature of progress, all agreed on the theory of the continual betterment of human affairs.[12] New Haven's Leonard Bacon emphasizes this sense of progress in his *Thirteen Historical Discourses.* Francis Parkman was a typically romantic historian whose writings were characterized by dramatic presentation of adventurous deeds. Parkman was interested in the early history of the continent coupled with woodland adventurers or battles.[13] Along with a nineteenth-century interest in social history such local New Haven historians as Bacon, Barber, Edward R. Lambert, and Edward E. Atwater gave attention to customs and everyday experiences.

The growth in this period of an awareness of American antiques generated a concern in the historical context of such items.[14] It is interesting to note that even though books themselves came to America in the early years of colonization it was well into the nineteenth century before libraries became significant centers for research in history.[15] In the mid-nineteenth century and shortly thereafter a new generation of historians came to the forefront, much further removed in time from the American Revolution. Consequently they had a more detached viewpoint. Also during this period many historians broke the spell of indiscriminate veneration of previous times.[16]

In the period before the Civil War it was difficult for American historiographers to appeal to the whole country. Because historians sought to serve the cause of their own areas, historical study as such came to a halt. Both authors of textbooks and histories experienced the emotion of sectional pride. The Civil War terminated for at least two decades all effective efforts to write American histories that would be palatable throughout the country. While many authors in the post-war period concerned themselves with the larger aspects of the Civil War, local historians were at work compiling community war records and regimental histories. An illustration of this type of assemblage is John Warner Barber's and Henry Howe's *The Loyal West in the Times of the Rebellion.* As the post Civil War animosity abated, a spirit of reconciliation arose among the people of the country. A drive to bring about national unity came with the celebration at Philadelphia of the centennial anniversary of the Declaration of Independence.[17]

During the last decades of the century a new scholarly and critical attitude became apparent in American historical writing. Previously the writing or editing of history had not been so much a profession as the pastime of gentlemanly scholars or literary individuals such as New Haven's Barber, Bacon, and the others. History, as a rigorous discipline, now became apparent in the courses of study at American colleges and universities.[18] Justin Winsor's *Narrative and Critical History of America* is considered an outstanding example of the new spirit of criticism of older historical writings. At the time of its preparation the long age of the amateur American historian was drawing to a close.[19] A considerable number of those who pursued their studies abroad assisted American historians in acquiring a new perspective toward the "scientific" potential of their endeavors. This attitude is reflected by Henry Adams' work at Harvard.[20] Henry Adams is said to have inaugurated the scientific school in

American historiography, for one reason Adams wrote American history was his desire to establish firmly all history as an exact science.[21] His fluency of style makes him a literary historian as well, and he wrote with vigorous critical standards and comparative objectivity.

To many students of American historical writing there is no interval that rivals in interest the period when Herbert B. Adams was at Johns Hopkins University. Among the ideas prominent during his time were the complex of thoughts called Darwinism and the associated belief that history is or should be a science. In 1881 Adams was placed in charge of the Historical Seminar at Johns Hopkins which he devoted to original investigations of American institutional history. In 1882 began the publication of the results of his research and that of his students with the initial issues of *The Johns Hopkins University Studies in Historical and Political Science*, the first series of its type in America. Charles H. Levermore's *The Republic of New Haven* was one of the early volumes in this series. During this period it was natural that American scholars considered history a science since science seemed to have triumphed in the thought of the nineteenth century. To some, science meant theory such as the natural scientists developed with Darwin's evolution. Others believed it meant complete objectivity. Most of the scholarly history produced in the United States since 1875 is based on objective fact.[22] Scientific historical writers of the latter part of the century believed that the fact was intractable. Coupled with the stress on accuracy came a great interest in procedures of critical analysis and also of verification.[23] There was a tendency among the newer historians of this period who were influenced by European universities to undervalue the contributions of previous generations of American historiographers.[24] In the latter part of the century American commercial historians compiled histories that stressed an area's business activity as well as its future growth.[25] In line with this general theme Edward E. Atwater provided for New Haven the *History of The City of New Haven.*

During the passage of an art or science from one culture to another a number of distinct periods of development may generally be noted. Initially the practitioners of the science or art are aliens. Next they are natives who have been educated abroad. Later another stage is reached when natives are educated at home by instructors who are either aliens or natives educated abroad. A last stage in this progression is when natives are taught by natives who have been educated at home. Between the years 1880 and 1900 the historical profession became firmly established in America. Shortly before the turn of the century there appeared in the United States two unique historical interpretations: Alfred Thayer Mahan wrote that sea power determines supremacy in international affairs and Frederick Jackson Turner espoused the fact that American history was shaped by its ever-expanding westward frontier. American historical writing had come of age. With the appearance of the scientific and professional historian we may, however, have cause to lament the passing of the nonprofessional historian. Perhaps scholarly training and learning may not always be adequate substitutes for experience but should be coupled with it.[26]

A survey of nineteenth-century American historical writing would not be complete without a review of local or regional historical societies and their contributions to the field. The organization of the Massachusetts Historical Society in 1791 initiated a new movement in America that greatly affected nineteenth-century historical writing.[27] The principle of willing association for the common benefit that encouraged the Rev. Jeremy Belknap and his associates to found the Society led to the founding of many similar organizations. The larger number of local and regional historical societies owe their existence to the dedication and interest of persons who have a sincere and often loving care for their particular locality.[28] For various periods ranging from approximately 100 to 175 years historical societies, mainly located on the Atlantic coast, have, as their principal reason for being, accumulated, preserved, made available, and published source materials of American history.[29] Early in its history the Massachusetts Historical Society began publication.[30] A majority of town histories produced in New England between 1792 and 1815 were published in the *Collections* of the Society.[31]

Early historical societies were somewhat restrictive in membership policies with a consequently limited participation of members of the community. In the middle decades of the nineteenth century one motive for the establishment of historical societies was a wish to investigate genealogical antecedents.[32] The interest in genealogy developed in part due to the wave of new immigration producing a desire on the part of many for native American exclusiveness. While New York merchants attempted to take trade from Boston, New York historians strove to claim a greater portion of the glory of the Revolution for their area. Historical societies served as a device in the conflict of local and national history as well as between local areas themselves. They could be described as bastions of localism. By 1860 the creation of historical societies had become a national mania. One way in which they gauged their accomplishments was by the quantity of documents they printed.[33]

The Connecticut Historical Society was incorporated in 1825, disappeared after four meetings, but was brought to life once again in 1839.[34] The New Haven Colony Historical Society was begun in 1862, and in 1863 a charter was granted by the State Legislature. On the Society's seal is the date of the area's settlement, 1638, and around its outer edge are the initial letters of the towns which comprised The New Haven Colony. The various homes of The New Haven Colony Historical Society in chronological order have been the New Haven City Hall, the third New Haven Connecticut State House formerly located on the Green, the old Insurance Building at one time on Chapel Street, the English Memorial Building on Grove Street, and now the English Memorial Building at 114 Whitney Avenue in New Haven. The reading and publication of papers on historical subjects was an early function of the Society.[35] As a result of this and similar activity elsewhere, coupled with increased college and university interest in history, the American Historical Association was founded in 1884 through the efforts of Herbert B. Adams and others. By the turn of the century historians from the educational world began to involve themselves in the older local or regional historical societies.[36] Franklin Bowditch Dexter, secretary to Yale University as well as professor of American History, showed a great interest in The New Haven Colony Historical Society. Volume III of that Society's papers published in 1882 contains four articles by Professor Dexter.

The American Antiquarian Society founded in 1812 by Isaiah Thomas at Worcester, Massachusetts, is national in perspective. The organization's library is a monument to one of the theories of how the country's history should be compiled, that is, state by state. The library now contains the best collection of state and local histories in the nation.[37] During the first half of the nineteenth century the gathering and preservation of manuscript sources of American historiography were the responsibilities of privately supported historical societies. In the second half of the century state legislatures, mostly west of the Alleghenies, began providing sums for the support of state historical societies.[38] The contributions of older historical societies to nineteenth-century American historiography are thus both significant and evident.

Leonard Bacon *circa* 1881

Leonard Bacon

Leonard Bacon, New Haven's "preacher historian," was for over half a century associated with Center Church. He was born on February 19, 1802, at Fort Detroit, Michigan, an important army post and fur trading center, where his father had been sent by the Connecticut Missionary Society to work among the Indians.

Bacon was the son of the Rev. David Bacon and Alice Parks Bacon. When he was six years old, the family moved to Tallmadge, Ohio, where in the nearby town of Hudson, Leonard Bacon and John Brown, later of Harper's Ferry fame, conducted a schoolboy dialogue. Bacon's father died when he was ten. After the family's return to Connecticut, he was placed in the care of an uncle, a Hartford physician. Young Leonard attended the Hartford Hopkins Grammar School and when he was fifteen years old entered the sophomore class of Yale College. He graduated in 1820 and subsequently went to the Andover Theological Seminary. After his graduation he spent an additional year there as a student licentiate and instructor in rhetoric.

Bacon was ordained on September 28th, 1824, as an evangelist by the Hartford North Consociation. He wished to become a missionary on the western frontier, but on the day following his ordination he received a letter from the First Ecclesiastical Society of New Haven's Center Church inviting him to their pulpit. After preaching fourteen sermons he was formally called by the Society to be its minister. He was installed with life tenure on March 9th, 1825, when he was twenty-three. Among the members of his congregation at the time were Samuel F. B. Morse, artist and later inventor of the electric telegraph; Noah Webster, the noted lexicographer; Senator James Hillhouse; and Eli Whitney, inventor of the cotton gin. An advanced intellectual level of preaching would undoubtedly have been called for. Initially Bacon did not live up to the expectations of the parish, for after some months a committee called upon him to request improved sermons.

In 1838 New Haven observed the two-hundredth anniversary celebration of its settlement. Since the organization of Center Church was coeval with New Haven's settlement, Bacon explored the early history of the area and the Church. A result of his studies was the delivery of thirteen historical discourses on Sunday evenings, which were later rewritten and published in a volume entitled *Thirteen Historical Discourses.* Publication gained for Bacon a firm position among the more prominent New England writers. (In line with his historical interests and after his resignation from the active pastorate he designed the inscriptions on the facade of Center Church that commemorate the founding of New Haven and the organization of the Church.)

Bacon was awarded the degree of Doctor of Divinity by Hamilton College and became a member of the Yale Corporation in 1839, and in 1870 Harvard made him a Doctor of Law. As time passed Bacon had grown in reputation as well as in the affections of the congregation. His parish was proud of his great influence within the city as well as of his reputation in ecclesiastical circles. Leonard Bacon was the sole and active pastor of the Center Church for forty-one years until 1866 and then pastor emeritus until his death in New Haven on December 24, 1881. When it was known that he was relinquishing the active ministry, Yale offered him a chair in its Divinity School. Bacon was acting Professor of Revealed Theology from 1866 to 1871 when he became Lecturer on Church Polity and American Church History, holding this position until his death. He married twice, first, in July, 1825, Lucy Johnson of Johnstown, New York, who died in 1844. In June of 1847 he married Catherine E. Terry of Hartford, who survived him. He had fourteen children.

Bacon was not essentially a great preacher. Though his sermons were solid and dignified they could ordinarily be quite dull, but on any occasion of great significance he was not found wanting. Leonard Bacon's written style was known for its clear expression of a practical understanding coupled with a tone of moral earnestness. He was a natural controversialist but engaged in no conflict which did not involve his conscience. Bacon was also well known for his wish to quiet controversy whenever possible. He was regarded by many as the most formidable polemical writer and speaker of his time in American Congregationalism. It might be said of Leonard Bacon that his chief contribution to the Congregationalist Church was his effort in arousing the denomination to self-consciousness and confidence in its polity. Bacon was known as a supporter of the New Divinity that promulgated the moral ability of man to choose between good and evil. This belief rapidly spread in the Congregational Churches of New England. Throughout his ministry he was occupied by works of moral betterment. He advocated the principle of abstinence from intoxicating liquors and at one time, based on the testimony of New Haven physicians, he showed that over one-third of the deaths above twenty years of age for several years in New Haven had been in one way or another attributable to overindulgence in alcohol. He was also concerned with the unsuitable conditions in the local schools.

He was a leader in the anti-slavery cause. Soon after coming to New Haven he helped establish a society for the improvement of colored people. At the Andover Theological Seminary he had supported the work of the Colonization Society as the one means then in view to solve the slavery situation. This society was organized in 1816 to help cope with the problem of the emancipated Negro. Its immediate goal was not so much the abolishment of slavery as the return to Africa of a sufficient number of freed Negroes to offset the annual increase. There were plans to establish a "civilizing" colony in which they could work out their own affairs. Such a community had actually been created on the west coast of Africa in what is now Liberia. The day before Leonard Bacon's installation at Center Church on March 9, 1825, the last sale of slaves occurred on the New Haven Green. In 1829 he submitted a plan for an academy in New Haven for colored youth but nothing came of it. He was well known for his support of gradual emancipation. Leonard Bacon believed in the opinion that held that since the property interest in a slave had been created by the community, the community should compensate for the loss an owner would suffer by emancipation of his slaves. During the early period of Leonard Bacon's public life he was particularly interested in the nonpolitical aspects of slavery. He fully believed that the ownership of human beings as merchandise was an abomination.

In 1839 the Amistad Negroes were brought to New Haven and their subsequent various trials became famous cases in American jurisprudence. The Negroes had been seized in Africa and then transported to Spanish Cuba and sold. While being moved by sea to another part of the island they mutinied and took the craft, a vessel named the *Amistad*. They then made their way to Montauk Point where the ship was apprehended by the United States Coast Survey. Spanish authorities claimed the Negroes. The question to settle was whether they should be set free or turned over to Spanish agents. The legal issues were ultimately decided by the United States Supreme Court with the Negroes being freed in 1841. Bacon was a member of the group which raised funds for the Negroes' defense and which also finally sent them back to their native land. His *Slavery Discussed in Occasional Essays from 1833 to 1846* contains many of his thoughts on this major question of the early and mid-nineteenth century. The book is said to have had a marked influence on Abraham Lincoln. Naturally it follows that during the Civil War he was a strong supporter of the national government.

Bacon's interest in church polity led to a concern with local government, evidenced by his extremely detailed paper entitled *Civil Government in The New Haven Colony* published in Vol. I of the *Papers of The New Haven Colony Historical Society* in 1865. Possibly Leonard Bacon was truly New Haven's nineteenth-century man for all seasons. When he was buried the only floral offering was a sheaf of ripened wheat as a symbol of the fulfillment of his life. The bell of the New Haven City Hall tolled in his honor.

In the preface to his *Thirteen Historical Discourses* Leonard Bacon writes that the interest and value of history depend chiefly on details. He also poses the question why the history of a parish should not be as interesting and important as the story of an empire. Bacon continues by saying that he stresses the virtues of the forefathers of New Haven because others had previously stressed their faults. He pursues this thought by pointing out that at the time of his writing people were more likely to forget virtues than opposite characteristics. (Bacon reminds us of the distinction between the Church of England from which many of the country's forefathers fled and the

Episcopal Church in the United States.) His work, Bacon says, is not, however, a book of preachings: the original sermons on which the text is based were extensively rewritten for this particular volume and his sources of information are generally indicated in the footnotes. He evidently considered this practice worthy of special note and mentioned the sheer amount of the work involved in preparing the volume as reason for a delay in its publication.[1]

In Discourse No. I concerning the *Causes of the Colonization of New England*, Bacon points out that early Spanish and Portuguese colonies in the Americas were founded on plunder and despotism. Ill-obtained wealth from the new world colonies contributed to the downfall of the two powerful nations. Bacon goes further and proposes that the singularly commercial purposes of early English settlement in Virginia led to a particular lack of success. He refers to England as the fatherland and mentions that the Puritan settlers of New England generally did not believe in secession from the Church of England but only wished a reformation. On the other hand he states that the settlers of Plymouth had actually renounced the Church of England. Bacon concludes his first discourse by suggesting that the early New England settlers were ultimately successful due to their high motives and holy inspiration.[2]

Bacon's Discourse No. II, *The Foundations Laid in Church and Commonwealth*, begins by extolling the virtues of New Haven's founding fathers and describes how they decided initially to be governed by the rules of the Scriptures. It then goes into great detail concerning the organizing of both church and civil state, coupled with a six-point defense of the New Haven colonists against charges of fanaticism and bigotry. Bacon mentions that the early settlers believed that church membership was necessary to the exercising of civil power because it was considered a certification of character. Bacon also, gratuitously, informs the reader that never were the universities of England better governed than when under control of the Puritans.[3]

In Discourse No. III, *Ecclesiastical Forms and Usages of the First Age in New England,* Bacon traces early New England church practices, pointing out that a clergyman in America is a minister who makes the ministry his profession and that while others may preach and be ordained if they pursue secular callings they are not clergymen. Bacon states that families should worship together—the earlier separation of men from women and both from children had been a mistake. He suggests a reason contributing to the known reluctance of early settlers to leave New Haven was that they did not wish to abandon family graves.[4]

Biographies are treated in Discourse No. IV, *Specimens of Puritan Ministers in The New Haven Colony.* The discourse covers in detail the ministers Peter Prudden, John Sherman, Thomas James, Samuel Eaton, and William Hooke. With the exception of Hooke all came with John Davenport from Boston to Quinnipiack in 1638. Bacon describes Prudden as distinguished by fervor and power, Sherman as characterized by wisdom and kindness, and James as having the reputation of an eminently holy man. He justifies Hooke's forsaking New Haven and returning to England in 1656 in a detailed defense, and he also speaks of Hooke as a good man.[5]

Discourse No. V covers *John Davenport in England, in Holland, and in the New England Synod of 1637.* Here Bacon provides an interesting footnote comparing differing authorities as to the details of John Davenport's Oxford education. One source states Davenport attended Merton College and later Magdalen Hall while another says he attended Brazennose College.[6] Bacon reviews the experiences of Davenport in both England and Holland, and also comments on English church history during the reigns of Charles I and II. In discussing the Anne Hutchinson incident in Massachusetts and the consequent New England Synod of 1637 Bacon makes the following commentary on human nature:

> There are certain opinions which always come forth, under one form or another, in times of great religious excitement

to dishonor the truth which they simulate, and to defeat the work of God by heating the minds of men to enthusiasm, and thus leading them into licentiousness of conduct.[7]

In this discourse Bacon also advances the concept that complete independence from England was possibly in the minds of some early New Haven settlers.[8]

In Discourse No. VI, *John Davenport and Theophilus Eaton the Founders of a New Republic*, Bacon states that both men possessed intellectual superiority and unquestionable moral worth, and points out their strictness in the administration of laws.[9] In a related footnote we again feel the wisdom of Bacon's teaching:

An association which undertakes to pronounce the law no law . . . is likely to do more harm, by teaching people to despise all government and magistry, than it can do good by any philanthropic endeavors.[10]

Bacon here reminds us of The New Haven Colony's record of scrupulous justice towards Indians as well as the absence of frivolous or extravagant legislation, and he notes the Colony's zeal for education.[11]

The interest in the founders of New Haven is continued in Discourse No. VII, *John Davenport in His Old Age*. Here Davenport's stress on education is reviewed. Bacon gives as the reasons for the creation of New Haven's outlying villages the defense of those living away from town, the convenient maintenance of the worship of God, the provision of schools and civil order, and mutual helpfulness. He praises the protection of the regicides (the judges at the trial of Charles I) by Davenport and New Haven. New Haven's sadness at Davenport's departure for Boston to spend his latter years is well presented. Bacon refers to the appendix as containing previously unpublished source material dealing with Connecticut's Governor Winthrop—that is, he shows an interest in research.[12]

Discourse No. VIII deals with the *Nicholas Street* as a symbol of the passing of the first generation of settlers. Bacon notices the decline in the last half of the seventeenth century in the respect people had toward the ministry compared to that which they had had for Davenport and his colleagues. He also comments that the power of religion itself was declining during this period because of the growth of selfish and narrow feelings and the decay of public spirit.[13] Included among the many Indian problems of the period was King Philip's War. Bacon's thoughts on armed conflict are explicit: "It demoralizes and barbarizes the people" and again, "When war in a righteous cause, war for liberty and for existence, rouses a people to enthusiasm, it makes religion not its ally only, but its handmaid."[14] In this discourse Bacon once again salutes those who have lived in the past when he states that the toil of early generations is enjoyed in later times.[15]

The next Discourse, No. IX, covers the period *From 1684 to 1714, James Pierpont*. These are the dates of Pierpont's ministry at New Haven's Center Church and include the time of the founding of Yale College. The section contains a great deal of New Haven and Connecticut church history. Bacon observes that in addition to the demoralizing effects of Indian wars on the churches that the increased political activity of the times contributed to a lessening interest in religion. An interesting point is made that after the absorption of The New Haven Colony by Connecticut the next two governors of Connecticut, Governor Leete and Governor Treat, were from the former area of The New Haven Colony. Bacon reviews details of the founding of Yale as well as the writing of the Saybrook Platform that contained suggested details of Congregational ecclesiastical organization.[16] Bacon, the historian, was trying to be honest. A footnote reads: " . . . somewhere . . . but I am not able . . . to turn to the passage."[17]

From 1714 to 1740, Discourse No. X, includes the earlier part of Joseph Noyes' ministry at Center Church. In this period the so-called Great Revival challenging the older order of the established churches began. Bacon presents both historical fact and his own feeling concerning this movement:

> One of the first symptoms of disorder, was the springing up of a corps of lay exhorters, untaught, uncalled, self-sent, who usurped the function of preaching the gospel, and brought themselves into collision with the instituted ministry and the organized Churches.

"These things were signs, not of the revival of religion, but of its decay."[18]

Discourse XI, *Extravagances and Confusion*, covers the period of the schism in New Haven's Center Church resulting from the Great Revival. Before Bacon provides the details how agitators of the period produced dissatisfaction within established churches, he advances the concept that the Rev. George Whitefield, a prominent leader of the English revival movement, assumed American churches had reached the same plane of unresponsiveness to religion as he contended prevailed in England.[19] A footnote in his section reminds us of a common nineteenth-century method of gathering historical data when Bacon refers to obtaining information dealing with Whitefield's preaching from an elderly New Haven resident.[20] And he reveals his respect for research based on documents:

> [Mr. Noyes] left behind him no published works, and as none of his manuscripts are now known to exist, it is impossible for us to form any just estimate of his intellectual powers and attainments.[21]

Bacon's feeling for the people of New England is made clear by the following description of its soldiers in the French and Indian Wars: " . . . not wretched conscripts from a wretched peasantry, nor the miserable sweepings from the streets of cities, but hardy freeholders and their sons. . . . "[22]

Discourse No. XII is concerned with *Chauncey Whittelsey and His Ministry* at New Haven's Center Church and includes the period of the American Revolution. A passage in this section seems rather familiar:

> They [the governing authorities of Yale College] were alarmed by the growing propensity among the students to violate not only the rules of the College, but the law of the land, by running away from the appointed place of worship to the separate [non-conforming] meeting.[23]

Bacon discusses the strong influence exerted for independence by the churches, other than the Episcopal, during the revolutionary period. He takes particular pains to exclude the Episcopal Church from criticism by pointing out that it was for many people the church of their homeland. He also informs us that since this church gained ecclesiastical independence during the Revolution it benefited from the struggle. Lengthy quotations from orations delivered at Whittelsey's funeral and on the following Sabbath point out one method of nineteenth-century historical space filling.[24]

The concluding Discourse No. XIII is *James Dana at Wallingford and New Haven.* Dana was a minister at Center Church. While this discourse contains the customary amount of church history, it also provides Bacon with a place for reflection on historical presentation:

> As we approach the close of this history, and begin to touch upon the doings and reminiscences of the living, our views must be more cursory, and we must advance with increasing rapidity.[25]

In this section we once again find the memory of another used as a reference source. Bacon discusses a prerevolutionary sermon delivered to the legislature by Dana based on a description given by one present at the time.[26] And he once more cites the deteriorating effect of war on religious interest: " . . . the disastrous and demoralizing influences of that [revolutionary] long conflict were felt most powerfully in all the

Churches. . . . " Bacon then takes the opportunity to advance the theory of the progress of civilization by making this comparison: "Let us thank God, not that we are better than the men of those [earlier] days, but that we live in better times."[27]

Another expression of this sentiment appears in the following statement describing relations between North Church and Center Church in the early years of the nineteenth century: " . . . and better days were enjoyed in New Haven than had ever been known here before." The theme is echoed in the following: "While I have felt the impulses of that natural enthusiasm which admires whatever is venerable with antiquity . . . the golden age is not in the past but in the future." And again,

> You can always find men who seem to think that the golden age was somewhere from fifty to two hundred years ago, and that ever since that indefinite point in the past, the world, and the church too, has been degenerating. They are not ordinarily very well read in history, but they have a strong impression, that in those good old times everything was very nearly as it should be.[28]

Bacon mentions the art of printing as a great ally in the diffusion of knowledge.[29] In the following he once more restates his case: "The scheme of Divine Providence is one, from the beginning to the end, and is ever in progressive development."[30]

The lengthy and detailed appendix of Bacon's work is in essence a miniature collection of New Haven source material. It contains such miscellaneous information as a description of the 1640 New Haven Meeting House taken from a record of early proceedings of the New Haven General Court and the copy of a will probated in New Haven during 1639-1640 with a most interesting inventory. Leonard Bacon in writing this volume provided students of New Haven's past with a detailed church history coupled with an examination of its ministers. He has also given a good general history of seventeenth-, eighteenth-, and early nineteenth-century New Haven. In essence the book is a history of New Haven's Center Church prepared in enormous detail and depth by a man associated with it for over fifty years. The history of the New Haven area is built around the central theme of church history. Bacon's devotion to his church is evident, as is his reverence for the ancestors of nineteenth-century New Haven. No similar history was prepared before his book was published, nor has one of equal magnitude or value been written since. *Thirteen Historical Discourses* makes an important contribution to New Haven historiography. One feels and senses the tempo and pace of Bacon's New Haven from its founding in 1638 to the 1839 publication.

Slavery was one of the dominant issues of the nineteenth century. It compelled Leonard Bacon's attention and he became engrossed in its problems. A detailed examination of *Slavery Discussed in Occasional Essays from 1833 to 1846*, published in 1846, provides an insight into Bacon's personal feelings. The book suggests methods for the solution of this then emerging American dilemma, and reveals trends in local and national opinion. At the beginning Bacon makes clear his intense interest in the slavery question.

> Several years before commencement of the Anti-Slavery agitation on this side of the Atlantic, it so happened that I was led to consider, with some care, the condition and prospects of the enslaved class in the United States. From that time to the present, no subject not immediately connected with my official duties or my professional studies, has occupied so much of my attention.[31]

Bacon calls attention to the fact that the reader may find some differences between the opinions given in his earlier comments and essays and in his later ones. But he was more interested in truth than in consistency. The essays do not attempt to prove that slavery is wrong. If an individual did not believe in the wrongness of slavery, he could not be changed by argument. Bacon continues that if slavery as it then existed in the United States was not wrong, nothing was wrong, but he also stresses that the unjustness of slavery was one thing and the way to rectify it another. The essays, Bacon says, primarily concern the way in which the wrong of slavery might be corrected.[32]

The first essay, entitled *Slavery*, is dated 1833. This is initially a comment on certain letters dealing with slavery addressed to the Cumberland Congregation in Virginia by J. D. Paxton, a former pastor. Bacon relates that Paxton had felt it was his duty to make his slave families free as soon as it could be done with a reasonable prospect of improving their condition, and he had sent his slaves to the colony at Liberia in 1826. Bacon mentions Paxton's comments on the folly of a congregation which believes a minister has acted imprudently when it takes offense at his preaching or conduct. He praises Paxton for a lack of bluster in his writings and also for his endeavors to instruct and convince slaveholders who believe there is nothing wrong in slavery. Stating that he does not endorse everything Paxton had written, Bacon turns to his own thoughts on slavery. Slavery is an artificial relation by which one is invested with property in the labor of another, to whom by virtue of such relationship he owes the duties of protection, support, and government, and is owed in return obedience and submission. The right the master has in his apprentice is actually the natural right of the father transferred, within certain limits, for the convenience and by the consent of the parties. On the other hand, Bacon continues, the relation of master and slave is the work of human legislation and has no foundation in nature.[33]

Bacon attacks the position of the adherents to slavery who tell others that the Scriptures justify their stand. Moses did not sanction slavery and Mosaic statutes respecting the relation of master and slave were modifications and amendments of previously existing ancient laws intended to assist slaves. Although Moses did not approve or sanctify slavery, neither did he move to abolish it immediately. He first tried to relieve the helpless and protect the defenseless. Bacon continues that it does not appear that Christ lived in a slaveholding country and that there was nothing in His personal history that can be considered as positively touching on the subject. As for the apostles, they said nothing in vindication of slavery while regarding the condition of slaves with sympathy. Bacon points out, however, that immediate emancipation on the part of slaveholders was not a condition for membership in apostolic churches.[34]

Bacon strongly presents his view that the mere fact of slave ownership should not exclude a man from the communion of the church. The crime is not in buying slaves, but in the purposes and views with which the purchase is made: a purchaser of slaves with any other view than to do them all the good he can is an offender. In the conclusion of the essay Bacon moralizes that the man who emancipates his slaves and places them where they will be truly free gives testimony against slavery which the consciences of others cannot resist and which will also give him peace of mind in death.[35]

Bacon's second essay in this volume is also dated 1833. *The Abolition of Slavery* comments on and reviews a collection of lectures dealing with slavery by Amos A. Phelps, Pastor of Pine Street Church in Boston. Bacon points out that Phelps is a member of that class of philanthropists who insist on what they call the immediate and complete abolishment of slavery. Bacon states his own feeling that abolition in almost any form is better than perpetual slavery. He then advances the thought that immediate emancipation of slaves in the United States would be considerably less beneficial and less equitable with regard to the slaves themselves than a more gradual change in their status. Phelps' feeling that a master has no right just to set former slaves adrift is reported. Bacon reveals his own viewpoint that slavery should be abolished immediately and then slaves emancipated gradually when they are in proper condition to be set free.[36]

Bacon's 1836 *Present State of the Slavery Question* is a commentary on the book *Slavery* by William E. Channing.

While touching upon Channing's thoughts, Bacon chiefly reveals his own personal concepts. The most important effect of anti-slavery agitation to the present has been to drive the small section of the southern community who favored its abolition into the camp of slavery defenders. Further, the fanaticism of the South is stirred by politicians who seek southern unity in national elections. Northern anti-slavery societies by stressing immediate and unqualified abolition tend to divide the north where all do not in fact agree on the stress for immediacy. On the other hand, southern agitators by their complete defense of slavery tend to unite the north. Bacon believes that Channing's book is well-suited to help bring about reconciliation of contrary viewpoints because of its sound presentation and that it will thus contribute toward a final triumph over slavery. Bacon additionally attacks the view that slaves must really be content, since their recorded crime rate is low, by pointing out that the master usually is both judge and jury and consequently courts and their records do not meaningfully enter into the picture.[37]

In 1836 Bacon prepared the essay *Slavery in Maryland*, reviewing a series of letters addressed by Professor E. A. Andrews to the Executive Committee of the American Union for the Relief and Improvement of the Colored Race. He comments on Andrews' report of conditions which reveal that slave labor employed in agriculture has long since ceased, with few exceptions, to be profitable in Maryland. This refutes those Southerners who claim the great comparative profitableness of slave labor in agriculture. Bacon continues by suggesting that if slave labor should become equally unprofitable compared to free-labor in more southern states there would be a greater number of people in such areas who would be more inclined to end slavery. Basing his comments on Andrews' letters, Bacon reflects that the great increase throughout the union of the free colored population is proof of a tendency toward emancipation. Surveying the entire Union, no class of population has increased in his time so rapidly as that of the free blacks. Andrews comments that the labor of free blacks is not considered as valuable as that of whites. Possibly this point is brought forth to quiet fears of job competition among segments of the white population. In line with this possibility of allaying fears Bacon points out that colored people tend to multiply rapidly as slaves, when they are raised as a crop, but when free the normal checks and balances on population will operate.[38]

Next is an 1845 *Letter to the Editor of the Philadelphia Christian Observer* written by Bacon. This is a protest against being misquoted. In the process of correction Bacon again states his philosophy that slave owning is not of itself a sin but that the conduct of the master and his feelings toward slavery must be investigated before judgment is given. He expresses his feelings about a segment of the white population of the south in a complimentary fashion: "I believe that thousands of the southern people are a great deal better than their laws are."[39]

Bacon's *The Collision Between the Anti-Slavery Society and the American Board* (i.e., for Foreign Missions), written in 1846, defends the Board. Once again his familiar views are brought forward when he opposes the Anti-Slavery Society's condemnation of the act of slave ownership without an accompanying investigation into the exact conditions. The Board proposes and Bacon agrees that every individual instance of slave owning shall be judged on its own merits. This controversy was brought about since some missions of the Board had taken into their churches Indians who held slaves. Bacon makes the following statement about slavery: "The institution is entirely and essentially barbarous."[40]

Bacon then touches upon the fact that the apostles had in their churches both masters and slaves, although the apostles as subjects of the Roman government had no political power over the laws of slavery. In our free country, however, there is no imposition upon the clergy of Roman law and enforced silence as was the case with the apostles. We are briefly brought back to the present and somewhat ·humorously by Bacon's comment that a slaveholder could make more money by selling his slaves and investing the proceeds in the railroad between New York and New Haven. Bacon reveals his views on the church and the slaveholding question in asking: " . . . is it not the province of the church to settle such questions?"[41] And again, "Christianity and the church recognize the slave as a man, an immortal spirit, a creature having rights, his master's equal before God."[42]

While New England Congregational churches have no direct ties to southern churches they actually are of the same great family and so should use their influence on the slavery question with the southern churches. Bacon summarizes a viewpoint on the question of the southern people with this thought:

> The true problem for anti-slavery philanthropy is, how to effect that change in the minds and hearts of the southern people—that change in their judgments and affections—out of which the legislative abolition must proceed.[43]

In this volume Bacon repeats again and again that he believes the act of owning slaves is not a sin but that the conditions of ownership and the ultimate intent of the owner must be taken into consideration. He proposes that slavery be abolished but that emancipation take place only when there is a decent place for slaves to go and a livelihood available for them. The church in the south should be a leading force in such a program. The writer of this survey has no present interest in the various authors Bacon has commented upon but only in Bacon's views and method of presentation as revealed by his own statements and discussions. Here is an important contribution toward New Haven historiography, showing how New Haven's leading churchman of the nineteenth century felt and how he influenced his fellow townsmen on the topic that ultimately led to the Civil War. Invaluable background material for a better understanding of early and mid-nineteenth-century New Haven is contained in this collection of Bacon's *Slavery Discussed in Occasional Essays from 1833 to 1846.*

Another significant interest of Leonard Bacon's was in the early government of New Haven, shown by several sections of *Thirteen Historical Discourses* and more concretely in a paper read before the New Haven Colony Historical Society on January 26, 1863. *Civil Government in The New Haven Colony* was published by the Society in Volume I of its papers in 1865. In this rather detailed study Bacon makes the point that New Haven's early settlers had no commission or charter from the English Crown nor from any other human authority. Consequently they felt themselves free to create by common agreement a government that would be in their own collective judgment the one best adapted to the specific purposes for which they had come from England.[44] Bacon then turns to what is evidently a major purpose for compiling the paper, a definition as to the times when the original settlers of New Haven created compacts for the transaction of their business as a commercial and emigrant company. He appears mainly interested in the formation of the plantation covenant as distinguished from the later church covenant. This plantation covenant is referred to as being created on the first day of extraordinary humiliation which the group of free planters held after they came together. The term "extraordinary humiliation" apparently refers to a time when the colonists met in awe and great reverence for the Supreme Being. Bacon writes that many historians assumed this to have been at New Haven, but he believes that in order for the settlers to organize it must have been at an earlier date. In addition Bacon presents his belief that the plantation covenant must itself have been preceded by an earlier agreement of the settlers in the form of a business accord.[45] He then proposes that the members of the New Haven company no doubt thought it was impracticable to form a church as well as a civil organization on this first day of extraordinary humiliation.[46]

The theme of early New Haven organization continues to dominate Bacon's thoughts in this particular work. He comments several times on the apparent satisfaction of the early settlers with the provisional arrangements for regulating their own affairs. Not until the fall of 1639, and after the settlers had been at New Haven for over a year and a half, was the new civil government completely instituted and formally installed. The first laws of the early settlers were summed up by the statement "the word of God," and at the time all other systems of law were expressly excluded from the colony. Bacon suggests that these views amounted almost to declaration of independence, since a new government with a new system of jurisprudence was established. He continues to dwell on the details of early governmental practices by suggesting that limited suffrage in early New Haven (i.e., the double qualification of being both a planter and also a church member) was not so very different from various forms of limited suffrage in the early nineteenth century. In both periods the vote was restricted to those in whom the authorities assumed the ability to perform intelligently. Bacon displays a liking for Biblical parallels when he mentions that Ezra and his company departed from the river Ahava on the twelfth day of the first month to go to Jerusalem. He then points out that the farewell letter to the Government of Massachusetts—early settlers of New Haven had stayed in Massachusetts before finding a place of their own—was dated on the twelfth day of the first month. His continued praise of the founding fathers and his emphasis on religious themes is indicated by the summation of his feelings on an aspect of New Haven government.

> But I may say that when they covenanted to govern themselves in all their work of founding a Christian church and a Christian state by those rules of duty which they should find in the Scriptures of the Old and New Testaments, they only professed distinctly what all Christian men profess implicitly. Our age is doubtless much more enlightened than theirs; but even in this age the man who would profess that his religion is purely ecclesiastical, and has no control over his conduct as a member of society

and an elector in a self-governing commonwealth, would be regarded in all churches of all denominations as a very scurvy Christian at the best.[47]

Bacon's often mentioned reverence for New Haven's fore-fathers is evidenced in a statement that the colony's first governor, Theophilus Eaton, was the most suitable choice, whether New Haven's establishment is considered a commercial venture or a political experiment. In Bacon's praise of Eaton both the commercial and political aspects of early New Haven receive recognition.[48]

This paper of Bacon's was written at a much later date than the other two works of his examined. While a concern for early New Haven governmental practices is evident in *Thirteen Historical Discourses*, the extreme detail shown in *Civil Government in The New Haven Colony* exceeds that except in which the most advanced student of local history would have an interest. Bacon did make an important contribution to New Haven historiography in the paper by providing a chronology of the area's early government, but the document is not for the casual reader.

The above engraving in the opinion of my friends is a correct portrait of myself at this time Feb. 2d 1880, my eighty second birth-day.

John W. Barber.

John Warner Barber *circa* 1880

John Warner Barber

John Warner Barber, New Haven's "illustrator historian," was
born in East Windsor on February 2, 1798, and died in New
Haven on June 22, 1885. Barber was the second of six children
of Elijah and Mary Barber. His father was a relatively poor
farmer. When Barber was fourteen his father died and he
assumed support of the family. Early in life Barber became
fascinated by illustrations. His understanding of the range and
character of his own art was shaped by the pictures he enjoyed
as a child. An examination of his work coupled with a review of
American children's books of the early nineteenth century will
confirm this observation. Barber's interest in illustrations led
him to make sketches and when he was seven he made a
drawing to celebrate Lord Nelson's victory at Trafalgar.

At sixteen he was apprenticed to Abner Reed of East Windsor, possibly the most prominent bank note engraver of his time. Barber finished his apprenticeship in 1819 and in 1820 moved to Hartford where he continued work as an engraver. Although he lived in Hartford, Barber seemingly found more business in New Haven. This might have been due to the existence there of Yale College and also the presence of his fellow craftsmen, Amos Doolittle, S. S. Jocelyn, brother of the well-known portrait painter Nathaniel Jocelyn, and Alfred Daggett. In 1823 Barber himself moved to New Haven. His business included both copperplate engravings and woodcuts. He was of course influenced by his training as an engraver of bank notes and similar material, as well as by the general state of illustrative work during his time, and throughout his work the style and character of his illustrations remain just simple records of what he felt or saw. Barber was a good technician as well as his own designer and cutter. He was a man of deep religious feeling, and practically the only latitude he allowed himself for the display of imagination and the play of fancy was in his allegorical works. *The Bible Looking Glass* and *The Picture Preacher* are examples of such volumes. A rough estimate is that Barber had a principal part both as illustrator and writer or compiler of thirty-four books and that he assisted in another eighty-four reprints or new editions. He made major contributions to nine books in which his name does not appear. In addition, Barber did countless illustrations for almanacs, encyclopedias, technical works, and many other publications.

He showed his love for detail by keeping a diary from January 22, 1813, when he was fifteen, until 1884. During this period only two months were missed, January and February, 1857, when he was seriously ill. He also omitted two days after the death of his first wife on March 17, 1826. The diary, essentially of the line-a-day type, devoted at least four lines to Sunday, usually indicating the church attended—Barber attended churches of every denomination—the minister's name and his text and a summary remark on the sermon. The diary is a most remarkable record of Barber's life and work. When still quite young he had envisioned the idea of histories compiled from individual memories of those who took part in important events which occurred during the periods of American colonial and early United States history—the diary is perhaps a testimony to Barber's belief in the written word. In 1827 he produced his first history book, *Historical Scenes in the United States*, intended especially for children.

At one time Barber traveled from town to town in Connecticut, either on foot or with his horse and buggy, making a great many drawings of practically every town and village and their objects of historical interest. He listened to and recorded bits of local history. When winter came and snow limited his activities he engraved or cut his drawings and wrote from notes his *Connecticut Historical Collections*. This method of gathering material became Barber's customary practice. He traveled widely throughout the country and then returned to New Haven to prepare for publication the results of his travels. In this way he helped to counteract somewhat the prevailing provincialism of the times. He also corresponded with many individuals to obtain information and studied works already published as well. Barber issued various books on many sections of the United States. A considerable number are illustrated by wood cuts and copper engravings he made himself from his original sketches. Barber prepared several historical writings jointly with Henry Howe of New Haven who accompanied him on some of his travels. Howe's father printed the first edition of Webster's Dictionary and operated a bookstore in New Haven, where Henry Howe pursued his literary tastes. After examining Barber's *Connecticut Historical Collections* Howe decided he would devote himself to producing similar records. In 1842 and 1843 he toured Virginia with Barber to prepare for the *Historical Collections of Virginia* which first appeared in 1844 and under Howe's name alone.

Of special interest to south central Connecticut historians is Barber's *History and Antiquities of New Haven* and also his

John Warner Barber sketching

compilation *A History of the Amistad Captives.* In 1832 Barber and Amos Doolittle re-engraved Doolittle's well-known "Battle of Lexington." The first re-engraved edition of this print may be found in the 1831/1832 edition of *History and Antiquities of New Haven*, a volume subsequently enlarged and on several occasions republished. The book was Barber's first of a local historical nature and consists of an assemblage of historical, biographical, and descriptive material. Its acceptance encouraged him to begin the groundwork for his *Connecticut Historical Collections. A History of the Amistad Captives* is of interest respecting the slavery question during the first half of the nineteenth century and New Haven's reaction to it. The Amistad case introduced an excitement into New Haven's community life unknown since the Revolution, and Barber attended sessions of the Connecticut trials.[1] After personal interviews with the Amistad captives through an interpreter he published the results, along with related documents, in *A History of the Amistad Captives.* The book has an animated and gory frontispiece showing the killing of the Spanish ship captain. It also contains biographies dealing with thirty-six of the captives illustrated by silhouette drawings. Barber was an active abolitionist and supported Bacon's ill-fated plan for a Negro academy in New Haven. (In 1833 he gave up tobacco and in his writings always preached against the consumption of liquor, again relating him to Bacon)

From the beginning Barber wished to cover more than just local or state history. As time passed his horizons and themes widened. An example of this greater perspective is *The Family Book of History*, written with J. Olney. The book is international in scope. His daughter Elizabeth wrote poetry and appears as a co-author with her father of *Historical, Poetical and Pictorial American Scenes.* A trip to Europe in 1853 with Elizabeth resulted in the later publication of *European Historical Collections.* Barber's works show a painstaking method of assembling minute details, the importance of which as historical data is questionable. His collected volumes could be said to comprise mainly a huge local history of the nation. He was particular in his efforts to obtain the truth, but of course local color must have played its part. Barber's books were produced before the time of scholarly historical writing and in an age more interested in the graphic episodes of history than in academic examination. He thus preserved picturesque and informative material from which one may obtain the background and general "feeling" of the periods of which he wrote. *Historical Religious Events* was his first publication of a religious character. At a later date various of his other books on religious subjects were issued in one volume, *The Bible Looking Glass*. This work sold 175,000 copies in the United States. Barber's religious writings were characterized by both enthusiasm and faith.

Barber was married twice, first on September 15, 1822, to Harriet E. Lines who died on March 17, 1826, and secondly on February 27, 1837, to Ruth Green, who died on November 8, 1851. By his first wife, he was the father of two children, Mary and David Brainard, and by his second wife of two sons, John and James, and three daughters, Elizabeth G., Caroline T., and Harriet. Barber was one of the founders of The New Haven Colony Historical Society and one of its first directors. From 1864 to 1869 he was librarian of the Young Men's Institute of New Haven. Henry Howe described his office as one of confusion but yet with everything apparently in place. Barber usually worked by himself. All his later labors were enlargements and elaborations of earlier ideas and purposes. For his various religious works Barber tried to interpret religious truths by means of pictures and short discourses. In his historical writings he strove to present in simple form the most important and interesting events along with geographical and biographical material. He recorded many interesting views and preserved historical material which other writers considered of little importance but which he himself thought worthy of saving for future generations.

An examination of John Warner Barber's contribution to nineteenth-century New Haven historical writing must begin with his *History and Antiquities of New Haven*. The 1831/1832 edition predates the majority of Barber's works and concentrates on New Haven. The object of his book, he says, is to collect interesting historical items dealing with New Haven without giving much thought to sequence or with any particular attempt to furnish a well-organized volume. Barber adds he has paid particular attention to many interesting subjects usually passed over by those who write customary histories and who believe such matters trivial: no doubt considerable amounts of history have been lost by not preserving such miscellaneous fragments of information in written form. He believes that old newspapers are among the best sources for information dealing with earlier times. He notes changing historical perspectives by pointing out that what appears to be unimportant to historians at one period might be considered significant at a later date. Early in his work we become acquainted with his love of detail through what can best be described as an extensive description of the physical characteristics of New Haven harbor.[2] He follows by a depiction of the private residences of New Haven that well illustrate his affinity for local particulars:

> The houses are generally two stories high, built of wood in a neat handsome but not expensive style. Many of those recently erected, are however, elegant and stately edifices of brick and stone.[3]

The fact that Barber might be considered more a compiler than author is brought out by his incorporating near the beginning of this book a lengthy quotation by Ithiel Town on the details of Trinity Church on the Green of which Town was the architect. Additional examples of lengthy space-filling by the use of source material occur throughout the volume, for example by the inclusion of extensive details concerning June 4, 1639, the date the New Haven settlers laid the foundations of their civil and religious organizations. The tendency to fill space is also shown by Barber's extensive use of newspaper quotations. An unusually long single quotation gives the details of the British invasion of New Haven in July of 1779. In one instance almost twenty pages of the book are devoted entirely to newspaper passages. These quotations in addition to providing general background material do give specific miscellaneous information about the area's feeling pertaining to such matters as the proclaiming in New Haven of King George III's ascent to the throne—quite a community celebration—or the policies concerning the importation of Irish servants or the details of a small British raid on West Haven in 1781.[4]

Barber is not noted for having taken pains to establish his historical facts or for particular accuracy. He says that Elihu Yale, for example, was born in New Haven, whereas he was born in Boston. Writing in the early nineteenth century Barber assumed that perhaps the oldest copy of the *Connecticut Gazette* still extant was a 1757 issue; this New Haven newspaper, begun in 1755, was the earliest newspaper in Connecticut; and less than one hundred years after its founding it is difficult to believe that had Barber devoted any reasonable amount of time to searching he would not have discovered earlier editions. Again, Barber when writing on the British invasion of New Haven in July, 1779, states that Dr. Daggett was the Yale President, but Daggett had not discharged the duties of president since March of 1777. Barber informs us that the colonial painter, Ralph Earl, was one of Benedict Arnold's group which heeded the call to Lexington and Concord, but Earl was not in fact a member of the unit.[5] Later editions of *History and Antiquities of New Haven* contain no alterations or corrections in these and similar errors.

Barber's statements about Eli Whitney and his inventive genius give an example of the generally flattering tone he used when speaking of a distinguished local resident.

> The machinery of this manufactory, is ingenious and peculiar, many parts of which were invented by Mr.

Whitney. It is to this gentleman that the world are indebted for the introduction of a machine, for cleaning upland cotton which annually saves millions of property to the United States.[6]

Barber in addition displays a fundamental awareness of community needs by stressing that early New Haven was not short of bread as other colonies had been.[7] He demonstrates that he can be a realist when, for example, he points out that the conduct of some Connecticut residents was not of the highest order during the July, 1779, British invasion of New Haven:

> It is said, that some of the country people [who entered town after the British had left], were base enough to take advantage of the general confusion, and carried off goods to a large amount.[8]

The book contains a list of names and professions of New Haven inhabitants in 1748.[9] This reproduction of an earlier compilation amounts to a forerunner of the present series of city directories.

Footnotes in this volume are often incomplete; however, the illustrations compensate for any lack of order in the text's presentation or accuracy. They are quite literal and convey the appearance of Barber's time in depicting the harbor, Green, and other local views. This volume concludes, unlogically, with two poems both dealing with East Rock, reprinted from other publications.[10]

Because of its unplanned structure and lack of organized presentation, Barber's book had no sequential order. In view of his inaccuracies his general veracity is open to question, although the reprinting of older documents often acts in place of footnotes, and he contributes to New Haven historiography by pointing the way to important source materials. More significant is his preservation of the tone and substance of early nineteenth-century New Haven through his illustrations. These interpretations capture the spirit of his time, and in sum the book is acceptable as an early guide to the history of New Haven.

Barber's preface to his *Connecticut Historical Collections* provides an insight into the author's religious feeling:

> The power by which we recall past scenes, the rapidity with which they are brought in review before us, the faculty by which we can "range o'er creation," and dwell upon the past and future, demonstrates that man was indeed formed in the image of his Creator, and destined for immortality.[11]

He continues his previously noted praise of the past by stating that all things relating to the history of the Pilgrims are worthy of preservation. In 1838 Edward R. Lambert echos this viewpoint in his *History of The Colony of New Haven.* Barber displays local pride by noting that while Connecticut is a small state with reference in both geographical size and population it is second to none in virtue, genius, and enterprise. As in the preface to *History and Antiquities of New Haven*, Barber here again defends his insertion of events thought by some to be trivial. He reminds us that many items considered to be of little importance prove later of considerable value. He mentions that many events some consider too "marvelous" (thus unhistorical) to write about are included. He informs us, properly, that religious beliefs and opinions even when in error become part of the history of a people.[12] Barber then calls attention to the many illustrations scattered throughout this work. His defense of their accuracy indicates Barber's belief in their significance: "The numerous engravings interspersed through this work, were (with five or six exceptions) executed from drawings taken on the spot, by the author of this work." Once again, "Before any view is condemned as being incorrect, it will be necessary, in order to form a correct judgment to stand on the place from whence the drawing was made."[13]

In many instances the text contains extensive explanations of the scene illustrated. An example is the description of a view of West Rock:

The cut on the next page is a representation of the southern termination of West Rock and a part of the village of Westville, (formerly known by the name of Hotchkisstown,) about two miles N.W. from the state house in New Haven[14]

Barber attempts to please as large a group of readers as possible. He expressly apologizes to persons whose names are omitted and who feel they should have been included and also for possibly slighting some aspects of local town histories.[15] This volume, as with his previous work, again includes lengthy quotations. An example is the Preamble and Hartford Constitution of 1639. He repeats many of the same newspaper advertisements and notices which were included in *History and Antiquities of New Haven*. The "Great Shippe" legend is the same in both *History and Antiquities of New Haven* and *Connecticut Historical Collections*. There are extensive newspaper notices in the New London section. In the pages on Newtown tombstone inscriptions consume considerable space.[16]

The book contains many historical facts not conveniently available elsewhere at the time. Such are the details accompanying the description of the formation of the United Colonies of New England, composed of Connecticut, Massachusetts, New Haven, and Plymouth, in 1643.[17] Barber uses the Farmington Canal as a geographical reference point throughout the book. In the Simsbury section he notes that the river and canal are parallel. When speaking of the village of Tariffville in Simsbury he mentions that it is near the canal. A reference to New Haven County states that it is intersected centrally by the canal. While discussing Cheshire, he points out that the canal passes through the entire length of the town. Barber orients an illustration of Hamden, which included the canal, by mentioning the canal in the accompanying text.[18]

While Barber should not be included among the later nineteenth-century historians who sought to glorify New Haven uncritically, the following comments from this volume are noteworthy. New Haven is one of the most beautiful towns in the Union. There were "not in the Union a body of working men more distinguished for their general intelligence and morality, than are the mechanics of New Haven."[19]

It is interesting to find in the Woodbury section Barber clearly showing that his reference point is New Haven. He describes a Woodbury hill by relating both its size and physical appearance to New Haven's East and West Rocks.[20] Barber was indeed generally uncritical and had a tendency to find good nearly everywhere. In writing of Milford he notes that the town has many improvements and others are contemplated. Greenfield, near Fairfield, is the home of some of the best farmers in the state. Salisbury is one of the best agricultural towns in Connecticut and also contains very rich and productive iron mines. Bolton has slate mines of great quality. Few country places offer such possibility for further improvement as Ellington. "The 'Ellington School,' designed principally for boys from the age of eight years to sixteen inclusive, is a respectable institution, and has acquired a deserved celebrity." Chaplin has many valuable mill or factory sites.[21]

The New Haven section includes a wide range of materials. Here Barber mentions how the Dutch knew of New Haven before the English came and had referred to the place by the name of "Red Mount," no doubt because of East and West Rocks. Barber recounts the ignominious death of the last sachem or chief of the local Indian tribe, the Quinnipiacs. He was named Charles and froze to death near a spring at East Haven in the mid-eighteenth-century. Barber mentions the use of the Scriptures as law in early New Haven. He also points out that the original New Haven settlers were the most affluent company which came into New England.[22]

In his comments on the organization of New Haven's early government Barber refers to the plantation covenant being enacted at Quinnipiac, New Haven's first name. According to Bacon in his *Civil Government in The New Haven Colony* this was not true. Bacon strongly supports the view that the plantation covenant was created before the settlers arrived at Quinnipiac.[23] He vigorously defends this assertion through a thorough examination of the evidence, but Barber in his usual manner just restates the accepted story. Barber also promotes a local myth when he repeats the story that the Regicides, Whalley and Goffe, were buried on the New Haven Green along with Dixwell, their fellow judge of Charles I. This legend evidently never had any foundation in fact and was later completely refuted by Franklin B. Dexter.[24]

Barber had no interest in maintaining chronological order within his town histories. In the New Haven section he follows a discussion dealing with various aspects of nineteenth-century New Haven with a listing of its 1643 residents. A statement concerning The New Haven Colony's great commercial losses in its Delaware adventure is followed considerably later by an incomplete explanation of what he had previously referred to. After discussing several phases of early nineteenth-century New Haven, Barber mentions that the Rev. John Davenport removed to Boston in 1668.[25]

Barber frequently reminds us of one of his methods of gathering information. He refers to obtaining data dealing with the British invasion of New Haven in July, 1779, from a member of a local group who resisted the British at Westville. He procured information concerning the Indians at Derby from an elderly Indian living in Kent. A gentleman in Waterbury is thanked for his assistance in providing information on that town. Details of the British attack on Fort Griswold at Groton during the Revolution were secured from an eye-witness, as was the account of the July, 1779, attack on Norwalk. Barber relies substantially for his historical material on Killingly, Salisbury, and Sharon on the memories of residents. He acknowledges assistance from Edward R. Lambert, author of *History of The Colony of New Haven*, and a contemporary of Barber's, for material on Milford.[26]

New Haven's original jurisdiction included many surrounding areas. Consequently a considerable part of its local history is recorded in the chronicles of nearby towns. The opening pages on Derby's history provides a case in point in its references to the activities of early New Haven settlers. The size of ancient Connecticut towns is well illustrated by a passage in which it is noted that some early land purchases of Milford from the Indians now represent a section of Waterbury. Such extensive areas would apply to all towns belonging to the old New Haven Colony. These areas were in addition to New Haven: Branford, Guilford, Milford, and Stamford. Southold, Long Island, was also a part of the Colony.[27]

The present-day concern of antiquarians to save ancient landmarks is reflected in Barber's statement about an Indian camp and burying ground in Derby: "Mr. Stiles, of this place, purchased this field about forty six years since, of the Indian proprietors, and in plowing it over, destroyed these relics of antiquity."[28]

Barber makes comments which show that in his recording of seemingly endless facts he does pause to reflect on political organization and various customs. In speaking of early Milford he observes the following: "Considering themselves as without the pale of jurisdiction (as in fact they were until they united with New Haven in 1644) they combined into a little republic." His description of Waterbury includes this commentary on military rank:

> These perpetual troubles [fear of Indian attack in the early eighteenth century], and the necessity of a constant system of military discipline, made our forefathers a martial people, and even the humblest of military honors were held in the highest estimation.[29]

Barber by a lengthy quotation in the town of Union section projects us into the modern political age. He anticipates current thought and practice on the one-man one-vote concept.

> This town . . . furnishes a striking example of the inequality and injustice of the principle of representation in this

state, and of the prevalence of the "borough system" of England. Union, with a population of 752, and with a list [tax] of 17,000 dollars, has an equal representation with New Haven, which has a population of more than 7,000, and a list of 133,000 dollars; having more than nine times the inhabitants of Union, and paying nearly eight times the amount of taxes; and upon a more just principle of taxation, the difference in this respect would be more conspicuous.[30]

The Salisbury section contains the story of an Indian engagement coupled with a frank statement by Barber that his version was obtained locally and differs slightly from that of another historian.[31] Barber thus acknowledges versions of history other than his own. His volume in its entirety reinforces the belief that one of Barber's important contributions to historiography is his preservation of local scenes. He states that his illustrations are literal interpretations. Consequently, while no doubt somewhat influenced by his own feelings and interpretations, they give a guide to the appearance in the early nineteenth-century of the greater New Haven area as well as of the state as a whole. *Connecticut Historical Collections* is essentially a Connecticut guide book with historical and antiquarian overtones. The many details of early New Haven and its notable residents occur both in the New Haven section and also in the units dealing with other Connecticut towns. It is possible to compare New Haven's own pattern of historical development with that of other state areas. The work thus gives perspective and background to New Haven's history by placing it in the context of Connecticut history as a whole.

At the zenith of his writing Barber prepared *A History of the Amistad Captives*. This compilation contains particulars of the Spanish slave mutiny off Cuba on the schooner *Amistad* as well as details of the related Federal Court proceedings in Connecticut. Of especial interest are the reported events in New Haven where Cinque and his associates were imprisoned after they had been taken into United States custody off Long Island. Also of interest are the extensive efforts of New Haven lawyers and scholars to assist the Africans, as well as the relations of Cinque and his followers with New Haven townspeople and Yale students. In this volume's preface we again find a statement on Barber's methods of gathering information:

> A correct statement of the facts of this extraordinary case, is deemed desirable, and the compiler has availed himself of the facilities at his command, for the attainment of this object. Free use has been made of what Professor Gibbs, of Yale College, and others, have published respecting the Africans. The compiler has also had the opportunity of personal conversation with them, by means of James Covey, the Interpreter, . . . [32]

Barber states that Cinque is the undisputed leader of the self-freed Spanish slaves, and the officers of the government ship that took the Africans into custody off Long Island considered him dangerous. Cinque was brought to New Haven in irons. There are lengthy newspaper and documentary quotations of the period and a group of head profiles of Cinque and his followers together with individual biographies. This section also contains the following unique statement about Cinque. "In fact, such an African head is seldom to be seen, and doubtless in other circumstances would have been an honor to his race."[33]

A defense of Cinque as an individual begins to evolve when it is pointed out that he never owned or sold slaves. There is a clear endeavor to present Cinque in the most complimentary manner when Barber repeats the statement of a United States marshal that he understood Cinque had stated that he had himself been a slave trader and had been seized to satisfy a debt of his own. These supposed remarks of Cinque are no sooner presented than they are quickly disposed of by the comment that Cinque was no doubt misunderstood. Also, in support of the train of thought that some Africans did trade in slaves, the remarks of an individual who had traveled in Africa are presented. Among this assemblage of details are the feelings of American officers claiming compensation for preserving property that included Cinque and his followers. The officers represent that they will only present their final claims dealing with the Africans if such are delivered as property back to Spanish jurisdiction. In line with various assertions of nonsupport of the slave trade is the statement of Judge Judson that under existing law and circumstances the Africans could not be sold.[34] Barber includes extensive details of the protracted Connecticut legal proceedings. Since these are reports that shed little or no light on Barber's method of presentation or his views, they are not commented upon here.

Barber mentions the help given the Africans in the way of daily instruction in the English language and Christianity by various young men connected with Yale College. He then proceeds to present some details of the Africans' thoughts and customs with the following statement, in which he again compliments Cinque and his group: "I rely with confidence upon their statements [the Africans], since a long and intimate acquaintance with them . . . justifies me in saying that I regard them generally as men of integrity."[35]

Barber mentions that the Africans did not understand the basic tenets of democracy. They have a reported revulsion to cannibalism. Barber also informs us that in the area of Africa where Cinque came from a wife is made to feel inferior and seldom eats with her husband. He quickly adds that Cinque and his wife ate at the same table. What might be considered a unique support by Barber of Cinque's African culture appears when he reports that the Africans considered the silence accompanying American funerals as an indication of insensibility. Another instance of advocacy of Cinque and his followers is the statement: "Especially do they seem anxious to learn that they may read the Bible—this is the great desire of their hearts."[36]

Barber reports that at one time when the interpreted Sabbath services were not available to the Africans that Cinque conducted them himself. The Africans expressed the desire that some of their teachers should return with them to Africa so as to instruct them and their people at home. Barber concludes by stating that Cinque and his associates deserve sympathy and should also have protection.[37] The book was printed before the final legal determination of the case.

This volume provides the reader with a clear indication of Barber's feelings toward the slavery issue. In addition to the large number of facts and the comments of others one can readily trace Barber's affection for the Africans and his own anti-slavery views. One way to announce these views was to support the Amistad mutineers. This volume should be considered a significant part of New Haven historiography, reviewing an important series of New Haven nineteenth-century events. It helps record the sentiments of the town on the question which led to the Civil War.

and prowess they were driven back. Intent upon the destruction of this little band, the savages with increased numbers and redoubled fury, in a few days, renewed their attack, and were again repulsed. From a chaos of heterogeneous materials he formed a well organized community of freemen. "Like the Patriarchs of old, he was their captain, their lawgiver, judge, priest, and governor."

View of the General Hospital of Connecticut.

The following account of the State Hospital Society of Connecticut, &c. was politely furnished by Dr. V. M. Dow, one of the directors of the Institution. *

The General Hospital Society of Connecticut was chartered in May, 1826, no similar institution having previously existed in this state. To aid the infant undertaking, the legislature of the state appropriated the sum of five thousand dollars, and individuals from different parts of the state have contributed handsome sums, while the medical institution of Yale College pays a yearly stipend. With funds obtained from these sources, the society have erected a neat building on an eminence south westerly from the densely peopled part of the city; commanding an excellent view of the town and one, of which 11,534 were within the city limits. The area occupied by the city, is probably as large as that which usually contains a city of six times the number of inhabitants in Europe. A large proportion of the houses have court yards in front, and gardens in the rear. The former are ornamented with trees and shrubs; the latter are luxuriantly filled with fruit trees, flowers, and culinary vegetables.

The houses are generally two stories high, built of wood, in a neat, handsome, but not expensive style. Many of those recently erected, are, however, elegant and stately edifices of brick and stone. The public edifices are the college buildings, ten handsome churches, a tontine, pavilion, state-house, jail, four banks, a custom-house, and a state hospital. Besides these, there are ten printing offices, from which are issued a daily, and four weekly newspapers; and one weekly, two monthly, and one quarterly, religious publications, and the American Journal of Science and Arts, conducted by Professor Silliman.

View of the General Hospital of Connecticut.

The General State Hospital Society, was chartered in May, 1826, and the building was completed in July, 1832. It consists of a center and two wings, and its whole length is 118 feet, and its breadth in the center is 48 feet. The build-

View of the General Hospital of Connecticut. *Left, by J. W. Barber and from his* History and Antiquities of New Haven; *right, attributed to J. W. Barber and from Edward R. Lambert's* History of the Colony of New Haven

Edward Rodolphus Lambert

Edward Rodolphus Lambert, New Haven's "genealogist historian," was born in Milford on March 20, 1808, the son of Edward Allyn Lambert and Anne Bull Lambert. Lambert early displayed an interest in local history. When he was twenty-six he petitioned the Town of Milford and was granted the privilege of examining its old records. This concern with antiquities continued throughout his life-time. (While on a trip to England in 1838 to inspect records for an attorney, Lambert visited many historical sites and ruins, thus enhancing his antiquarian background.) Although he considered Milford his home, it is probable that he also lived in New Haven at some time. In 1849 or 1850 he moved to Bridgeport where he resided until his death on June 19, 1867. There Lambert pursued the profession of architect and later of surveyor. In November of 1864 he made with George Beckwith the original survey of Bridgeport's Seaside Park. He married Eliza Boothe of Wallingford in New Haven's Trinity Church on January 1, 1833. They had ten children: four sons, Edward Richard, Henry A., Roger and Alfred, and six daughters, Eliza Boothe, Anne, Helen, Mabel, Elizabeth and Julia. Roger and Mabel died in infancy; Eliza Boothe, Helen and Julia succumbed in early childhood. Lambert was buried in Milford.

In 1838 Lambert's *History of The Colony of New Haven, Before and After the Union with Connecticut* was published. He felt proud enough of this contribution to New Haven historical writing to send a copy to the British Museum in London. Lambert was also noted as a map maker and for his great interest in genealogy.

In examining Edward R. Lambert's *History of The Colony of New Haven* one realizes early that Lambert is a venerator of the past. His views about the founding fathers are clearly shown: "In fact, everything relating to the history of the colonization of New England is worthy of preservation."

> The discovery and settlement of America by Europeans, was an event of the greatest importance, and one which every true American, and particularly every descendant from the original colonists, will ever delight to contemplate.[1]

Lambert presents in positive and complimentary terms his own feelings concerning the character of New Haven's early settlers. They were highly respectable and the Rev. John Davenport and the Rev. Peter Prudden were in particular "genuine Puritan ministers." The wealth of the original settlers is also mentioned. Lambert stresses the importance of accurate history. He thanks the old Colony of New Haven for the foundations of the New Haven of his own day. Like John Warner Barber, he attaches great importance to rescuing from oblivion and placing in print obscure bits of local history. Lambert writes of his great labors in compiling his work and also states that he expects no adequate financial return for his efforts. He hopes that his example will induce others to make similar collections of local history in other areas of the country[2]

We are again reminded of his pride in and affection for the original settlers when he speaks of the founding in 1638 of the "flourishing Colony of New Haven."[3] As in numerous other nineteenth-century historical writings on New Haven, many and lengthy quotations of source material are included (but usually no adequate footnotes). Here again we find a favorite story of the venerators of New Haven's past. This is the account of the Regicides, Whalley and Goffe, being buried near Dixwell, their fellow judge of Charles I, on the New Haven Green. As has been previously noted, this tale was refuted by Franklin B. Dexter.[4] Lambert discusses New Haven's geography in detail.[5] There are signed illustrations in this book by Barber, but the greater number of scenes are not attributed to any artist or engraver. A close comparison of the signed views with those unsigned indicates that the majority, if not all, of the unsigned illustrations are also Barber's works.

The book contains separate sections for The Colony of New Haven, the Towns of New Haven, Milford, Guilford, Branford, Stamford, and Southold, Long Island. A section near the close of the volume, entitled *Sketch of Olden Times*, contains various odds and ends among other topics on church history, Thanksgiving celebrations, early standards of conduct, and style of dress and architecture. Possibly this was Lambert's method of providing general background material for more specific historical facts and events. But after his detailed glorification of New Haven's past one is surprised to find the following statement:

> . . . it may be remarked, that the tide of fashion, which overwhelms everything on its onward course, has almost effaced every trace of what our forefathers possessed or

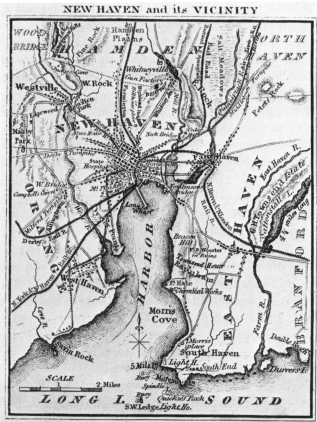

New Haven and Its Vicinity *circa* 1880. Drawn and
engraved by J. W. Barber

used in the way of dress, household furniture, or equipage, but whether the change which has taken place is "for better or worse," is left to the reader to decide.[6]

In the last section of his book, entitled *A Genealogical Sketch of the Lambert Family*, we learn of Lambert's regret that during the early part of the nineteenth century there was a lack of interest in the United States about ancestral history. He laments the lack of herald offices where the pedigree of families are traced and recorded. Lambert continues that there is satisfaction in knowing human lineage and that such studies help place man above the animals who but live and die with no record. He defends the inclusion of his own family genealogy by saying that it was not motivated by vanity but was published at the request of many of his friends—its incorporation did not increase the price of the book! We are also informed, not surprisingly, that the Lambert family is descended from high antiquity. The genealogical section concludes with Lambert's hope that others at a later date will continue his family's genealogy.[7]

Lambert's work contributes somewhat to New Haven history by providing the reader with a compilation of facts and antiquarian material, but worship of the past seems more important than a record of the past. The book was published in 1838, less than ten years after Barber's first edition of *History and Antiquities of New Haven*. It includes more information with respect to the Colony than Barber's. Lambert's work is also slightly more detailed than Barber's. A close examination of both books shows that Lambert made use of some of Barber's material. Lambert's *History of The Colony of New Haven* made a worthwhile contribution when published. Today it provides an insight into how one nineteenth-century writer thought and felt about local New Haven history.

Edward Elias Atwater

Edward Elias Atwater was born in New Haven on May 28, 1816, the son of Elihu Atwater and Julia Thompson Atwater. After graduating from Yale in 1836 he tutored a year for a family in Oldham County, Kentucky. In 1837 he entered the Yale Divinity School. On November 24, 1841, Atwater was ordained pastor of the Congregational Church in Ravenna, Ohio, a position he resigned on July 1, 1849. After a period of foreign travel he was installed on February 3, 1852, as minister at the Congregational Church in Salmon Falls, Rollinsford, New Hampshire. Atwater returned to New Haven in 1857 to undertake an assignment in the eastern part of the city. This activity resulted in the organization of the Davenport Congregational Church where he was pastor from April 22, 1863 to June

14, 1870. He continued to reside in New Haven pursuing his literary endeavors. Late in 1887 he went to Florida for the winter and there died, at Hawthorn, on December 2, 1887. Atwater married Rebecca H. Dana of Pomfret, Vermont, on August 9, 1844. Their only child, Elihu, died in infancy.

In 1881 Atwater's *History of The Colony of New Haven to its Absorption into Connecticut* was published. That undertaking led him to spend the last years of his life in editing, compiling, and writing sections of his major work, the *History of The City of New Haven*, published in 1887. This commercial history of the city was Atwater's most significant book as a source of information for today's local historian.

Atwater's *History of The Colony of New Haven* covers the period from the founding of New Haven up to and including 1664/65 when the New Haven Colony was absorbed into the Colony of Connecticut. Atwater states that he is certain many descendants of the early settlers will be interested in his book. In addition he hopes that descendants of later immigrants and those born in foreign lands but who now live in or near New Haven will also wish to know about the city's origins.[1] Atwater makes the following comments about historical presentation and source material.

> Reference has not always been made to the original authority, in confirmation of a particular statement. Such references may be useful to the specialist, but when frequent are annoying to most readers.

> Lambert [the author of his own *History of The Colony of New Haven*] says that Pruden preached in the afternoon [of the first day of the settlers at Quinnipiac], but does not give his authority. It was perhaps a Milford tradition, and it has inherent probability.[2]

Early in the book the author states that a history such as he is writing must begin with a detailed examination of England before the time of the initial emigration of the Puritans.[3] The first chapter of the book thus contains background material on both Tudor and Stuart England. Atwater's second chapter provides a summary of the Puritan movement in England. Like most other nineteenth-century writers of New Haven history Atwater quotes at length from documents. Chapter VIII includes detailed comments on the families of the early settlers and provides a background for later events.

The volume is a history of the New Haven Colony and consequently includes the early history of the Colony's other towns, Branford, Guilford, Milford, Stamford, and Southold, Long Island. Atwater makes the customary comment about the substantial wealth of the New Haven colonists. He then suggests that had they foreseen the later reverse emigration back to England in Cromwell's time, as well as New Haven's commercial misfortunes, they might have built less pretentious homes.[4] Here we begin to see Atwater more clearly as commentator as well as reporter. He observes that the confederations of both the New Haven Colony and also the United Colonies of New England (Connecticut, Massachusetts, New Haven, and Plymouth) were necessary to security and peace. Atwater states that in towns within the old Colony other than New Haven husbandry took more of the time and attention of the inhabitants than in New Haven: since these practices are not particularly interesting he will not comment on them at length. Atwater observes that within ten years of New Haven's founding it had a great many physical provisions for a civilized life. His remarks that the early colonists of New Haven were never advocates of religious liberty explains the general character of the settlement. "If the Puritans had been in power in England, they would have suppressed the ritualism of Laud as heartily as Laud punished non-conformity." And, New Haven's settlers "saw no other way of securing the end for which they had exiled themselves, than that of [religious] exclusiveness and intolerance." Atwater proposes, however, that possibly the religious excesses of the past might have been better than the opposite extreme exhibited in his own day.[5]

The author notes the just treatment of the Indians by the settlers. He mentions that one of the essential features of an early homestead was a brew house and adds that in early New

Haven beer was on the table as regularly as bread. The simple and regular life of the colonists, says Atwater, was favorable to health. Their social life had as its basis contemporary social life in England but naturally as modified by both Puritanism and emigration.[6]

Possibly the understatement of the volume, if not of all nineteenth-century New Haven history, is Atwater's suggestion that the "restoration of the Stuarts was not received in New England joyfully." This work also contains a suitable and concise epitaph for the Colony. "After two centuries, New Haven scarcely remembers that she was once a distinct colony."[7] The appendix provides a miniature reference library of reprints of source material, including the very detailed seating arrangement of New Haven's original meeting house.

Atwater provides the reader with a long compilation of facts and much background material on early New Haven. The scarcity and limited scope of his footnotes means that most of his statements must be accepted chiefly on faith. His book, however, provided latter-day nineteenth-century New Haven with a more detailed text on its early history than had been previously available. Consequently it made a valuable contribution in its time. Today it provides a wealth of miscellaneous information for a study of the city's origin. Atwater's comments supplementing his facts also give an insight into how a writer of the late nineteenth century viewed customs of an earlier time.

Atwater's *History of The City of New Haven* is certainly a vanity history in the truest sense. Despite this, it must be acknowledged that much general historical information is included. The following statement clearly shows that he is writing for the greater glorification of the city and its inhabitants.

> It is due to those who furnish the portraits with which the volume is adorned, to say that without the generous subsidy of these patrons it could not have been published.

To them, all who value the volume are indebted both for the possibility of its production and for the increase of its value by reason of these costly engravings.[8]

The history has thirty-nine chapters, nineteen of which and part of another are by Atwater, and an appendix which he compiled. (The sections he wrote will be commented upon here, and when the contributions of others are mentioned it will be indicated.) Many of the chapters were supplied by others than Atwater—lives of local lawyers, doctors, and dentists, for example. Innumerable biographies, the first of which is of David Wooster, New Haven's revolutionary hero, reveal the intent of the book to glorify and praise the City and its inhabitants as much as possible. The historical sections are also the work of many contributors beside Atwater.

Near the beginning of the book Atwater repeats the statement with which he concluded his earlier volume on The New Haven Colony: "After two centuries, New Haven scarcely remembers that she was once a distinct colony."[9] The reuse of the passage alerts the reader to the fact that Atwater will employ here a great deal of material from his previous history. The work is filled with many extraneous pieces of information such as the following.

A musket is in the possession of the New Haven Colony Historical Society which was captured with its owner, a Hessian, by Mr. Jonah Hotchkiss, who at the time had his last charge of powder and ball in his own gun.[10]

Among many random comments is one which gives some indication of Atwater's feelings on the slavery question.

It [the election of Abraham Lincoln to the Presidency] extinguished in the breasts of those who loved the institution of slavery, all hope of extending it into the virgin soil of the public domain by Constitutional measures.[11]

Chapter IV "New Haven During the War of the Rebellion," contains many accounts of the organization of New Haven military units for the Civil War. It also provides the following bit of Connecticut library history.

> This canvas chapel and reading room [of a Connecticut unit serving in Maryland] being found so useful, an association was formed of men from all parts of the State to supply Connecticut regiments with chapel—tents, books, magazines and newspapers, and generally to aid chaplains in promoting the moral and spiritual welfare of the soldiers.[12]

Chapter VI "Churches and Clergymen," is a lengthy but invaluable compilation on New Haven churches and their clergymen. Here, as in most other sections, the reader must take the writer's word for the majority of the information, for Atwater rarely indicates sources. Chapter VII deals with schools and has a great deal of information interesting to the local historian. This section also contains an odd statement that may be an advertisement.

> The building [the West End Institute] is situated so as to be on all sides open to the light; every room in turn receives the sun and it bears throughout a bright and cheerful aspect.[13]

Chapter XXXIV, "Traffic—Wholesale and Retail," as well as Chapter XXXV, "Productive Arts," appear to be commercial listings in historical settings. Chapter X, "Contributions to Literature," provides various miscellaneous literary items. Its concluding paragraph states that it is not a section of advertisements.

> New Haven has many contributors to literature who have not yet finished their work; but those whose names have been mentioned are all among the dead. Many more might be mentioned who have wrought in periodicals and

pamphlets; but these have produced bound volumes of greater or less magnitude and in various departments of literature.[14]

"The Periodical Press" is the title of Chapter XII. It contains a good historical summary of New Haven newspapers and similar publications, including those associated with Yale. The chapter has the following footnote which illustrates this book's general lack of informative citations. It is a reference Atwater uses to support certain aspects of Benjamin Franklin's interest in New Haven printing. "Those letters are extant, but so carefully put away by Governor Charles R. Ingersoll that, after diligent search, he has not been able to find them."[15]

A part of Chapter XIV, "The Practice of Medicine and Surgery," by one of the contributors, Francis Bacon, M.D., contains a more complete and informative use of footnotes than appear elsewhere in the volume.

A quotation from Chapter XXX, "Financial Panics," reveals some of Atwater's economic and political views.

> Since the panic of 1873 there has never been any expansion of credit so great as to threaten another explosion. Trade has seemed to have an automatic regulator, so that when too brisk it slows up of itself; and when dull, its dullness is in degree like the darkness of night, which is darkest just before day. If the banks profit by experience, and Congress shuns rash experiments and sudden changes, we may hope that the financial panics of the past may be the means of saving us from their repetition in the future.[16]

In Chapter XXI, "Streets, Avenues and Bridges," there is a Biblical allusion when Atwater refers to New Haven as having more entrances than there are gates into the New Jerusalem. A statement in Chapter XXIII, "The Post Office," provides an indication of the relative importance of New Haven in the latter part of the nineteenth century. Atwater describes the New

Haven Post Office as the first in Connecticut and the twentieth in the United States in the amount of mail handled. Henry Howe, who collaborated with Barber on many historical works, prepared Chapter XXVI, "Trees and Parks." Atwater uses Chapter XXVII, "Artificial Illumination," to promote the sale of gas. Just as railroads increased the demand for horses so perhaps will electricity stimulate the consumption of gas. A paid advertisement? Atwater displays in Chapter XXVIII, "Water Supply," the spirit of the civic-minded citizen when he states that under New Haven's plain is a plentiful supply of good water. The same spirit is continued in Chapter XXX, entitled "Health," by Professor William H. Brewer. New Haven is a healthy town with a relatively low death rate which may be attributed to New Haven's location and the character of its people.[17] Charles H. Levermore who wrote *The Republic of New Haven* is a major contributor to this book with Chapter XXXI, "Municipal History."

In writing and compiling this work Atwater made an important contribution to New Haven historiography. The *History of The City of New Haven* covers all aspects of New Haven development. In several categories, such as the biographies and the commercial listings, he furnishes unique and unusual material not elsewhere available. Lack of indicated sources leaves one to accept Atwater primarily on faith. More sophisticated works in both style and method of historical presentation have been published, but no other history of New Haven contains the wealth of material Atwater's *History of The City of New Haven* includes. It is also interesting to note in it Atwater's own observations in many fields. His personal comments help reveal the "tone" and spirit of late nineteenth-century New Haven. This massive volume of 702 large-size pages is a library in itself.

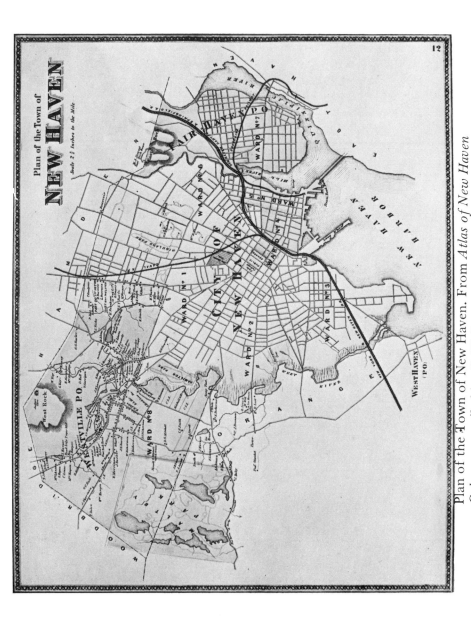

Plan of the Town of New Haven. From *Atlas of New Haven Colony*, compiled by F. W. Beers, New York, 1868

Charles Herbert Levermore

Charles Herbert Levermore, New Haven's first "scholarly historian," was born on October 15, 1856, in Mansfield. His parents were the Rev. Aaron Russell Livermore, a Congregational minister, and Mary Gay Skinner Livermore. His father's and mother's families had on both sides deep roots in Connecticut. After preparing for college at New Haven's Hopkins Grammar School he received a Bachelor of Arts from Yale College in 1879. Shortly thereafter he adopted the older spelling of the family name, that is, Levermore. He considered it the more historic form.

Levermore served for a time as principal of the Guilford Institute at Guilford. In 1886 he received his Doctor of Philosophy from Johns Hopkins University. He taught at the

Hopkins Grammar School in New Haven while completing his doctoral dissertation. It was published in book form in 1886 with the title, *The Republic of New Haven*. Prior to that time no history of New Haven had been written based on so much scholarly research and inquiry. Levermore also taught at the University of California and Massachusetts Institute of Technology, and he served as principal of Adelphi Academy in Brooklyn, New York. Later he was president of Adelphi College in Brooklyn, which he helped found. After retiring in poor health from the College in 1912, Levermore spent a year of rest and recuperation in the South and then concentrated on activities in behalf of world peace. He served as acting director of the World Peace Foundation, as secretary of the New York Peace Society and of the World Court League and League of Nations Union, as well as of the American Association for Internal Cooperation. Levermore assisted in organizing the League of Nations Non-Partisan Association, of which he was vice-president. In 1924 he was given the American Peace Award, created by Edward W. Bok. The publicity accompanying this award brought him international recognition. During World War I he was a member of the U.S. Public Service Reserve and after the war served as director of the Society for Promotion of Education Among the Russians.

Levermore was a prolific writer, but of special interest to this study is New Haven's first scholarly history, *The Republic of New Haven*, as well as the chapters, "The Town Government" and "The City Government," which he contributed to Atwater's *History of The City of New Haven*. Levermore was married in New Haven on September 4, 1884, to Mettie Norton Tuttle. The Levermores had six children: two sons, Charles Lewis and George Kirchwey; as well as four daughters, Mora (who died in infancy), Margaret, Lilian, and Elsa. Levermore, who had toured Europe and North Africa after receiving the American Peace Award, was preparing for a trip to the Orient when he died in Berkeley, California, on October 20, 1927.

The Republic of New Haven is one of the Johns Hopkins University Studies in Historical and Political Science edited by Herbert B. Adams. Levermore states that a purpose of his work is to depict the steady evolution of local government as well as to trace the influence of the church and to investigate the gradual differentiation between church and state. He will also observe the operation of political and social agencies. In addition he wishes to determine the permanent characteristics which compose New Haven's individually. These pronouncements of intent provide the reader with a general outline of the book's structure. Levermore comments that records of the Colony, Town, and City of New Haven were carefully examined and copies compared with originals—the age of the scientific historian had arrived for New Haven. He also mentions that local histories and their assimilation into larger state histories provide the building blocks.of history[1]

Levermore stresses continuity with the past in his first chapter, "The Genesis of New Haven." He provides background information on the Puritan movement in England as well as other information on New Haven's establishment and early government. The connection with the past is emphasized in a passage such as the following, dealing with military training days in early New Haven: "From time immemorial Englishmen have converted days for military practice into holiday seasons. . . . " Levermore continues in this vein by commenting that features of the teutonic township found their duplicates in the Town of New Haven. "Here were the cables, invisible, but stronger than adamant, that bound them not only to England, but to the wooded Germany of Tacitus and Arminius, and even to the faraway Aryan villages."[2]

Levermore again brings forth New Haven's ties with the past by informing the reader that the concept of the English city was more dominant in New Haven than in any other New England location. He even compares New Haven's late seventeenth-century provincial views on foreign affairs with those that might have come from a city-republic of ancient Greece. But Levermore is no sentimentalist and he is aware of change. He points out, for example, that the two creeks which provided boundaries for early New Haven have become in one instance the site of a sewer and in the other the location of a railway track.[3]

Levermore emphasizes early New Haven's distinctive features by describing its relatively greater per capita wealth compared with other New England settlements. He also mentions that the original government gradually came into line with practices of the other colonies. The church in early New Haven deemed as one of its functions the purification of society, which meant even including those who were not church members. In connection with the power of the church it was forbidden to eat or drink with excommunicated individuals. Such was the authority and way of the early established religion.[4] The following comment shows that Levermore considers the revolutionary period to have been a time when New Haven began to realize that there were important affairs other than merely local problems.

From oyster laws, from restraints upon unruly geese, and from the marking out of new highways, the drowsy Town Records suddenly wake up to the din and confused alarms of the Stamp Act and Boston-Port-Bill time.[5]

Levermore states that the New England Town Meeting was generally near the heart of the insurrection and that in New Haven this was true. He comments upon a significant area as he discusses the political factions existing when New Haven became a city in 1784. On one hand were the staid conservative families, known usually as the town-born, and on the other the younger enterprising businessmen, called the interlopers. Levermore believes that this division dated from a revival of New Haven's commerce in about 1760. David Wooster of revolutionary war fame, Senator James Hillhouse, and Roger Sherman were all considered interlopers.[6]

Levermore indicates briefly his own anti-slavery sentiments by presenting New Haven's abolitionists in as favorable a light as possible.[7] His book also contains a fine summarizing comment on the Farmington Canal.

> It cut deeper into the financial prosperity of the place than into its soil. The Town-Meeting, which enthusiastically approved of the project, was appropriately held on the first of April, 1822.[8]

The city placed $100,000 of borrowed money into the project before its failure, with the principal result of the investment being a rise in the tax rate.

Levermore straddles the fence in discussing the relationship of Yale and New Haven. He maintains that the college brought to New Haven an academic atmosphere unfavorable to normal development. This was because the large Yale-oriented segment of New Haven's population cared only for the institution and little or nothing for the political unit. This indifference was more significant when the town was small and did not increase proportionally as the area grew. After expressing those negative thoughts Levermore performs an about face when he suggests that what as a university town New Haven has lost in one direction it has gained a thousandfold in others. He maintains that by its identification with Yale the area has favorably projected itself.[9]

Toward the end of the volume Levermore again stresses continuity.

> The spirit of moderation which has generally been dominant in New Haven has ensured to the municipality a consitutional development that is, at least, continuous.[10]

The concluding Chapter IX, "The Present Municipal Administration," contains a detailed summary of New Haven municipal affairs coupled with suggestions for improvements as Levermore interpreted them.

The Republic of New Haven, clearly a scholarly endeavor, introduces New Haven history to the academic process of verification and analysis of source materials. It provides an examination of the European roots of New Haven history. Levermore's objective approach to all aspects of New Haven's past is refreshing. One does not feel that a preconceived glorification of olden times will influence the author's presentation and interpretation. Without Levermore's volume one might feel that all of New Haven's major nineteenth-century historical writings were really only acts of piety.

Summary of New Haven Nineteenth-Century Historiography

Before the writings of the five authors considered here there were no New Haven historical works of any consequence. This is true unless one includes passages or sections with reference to New Haven in earlier publications of greater scope, such as Cotton Mather's *Magnalia Christi Americana* published in London during 1702, or Benjamin Trumbull's two volume *A Complete History of Connecticut*, which appeared in 1818. As a result there was a need in the nineteenth century for writings relating to local history. The contributions of Leonard Bacon and John Warner Barber are more significant than those of Lambert, Atwater, or Levermore. There were no other nineteenth century historians of importance writing about New Haven.

When Lambert in 1838 published his *History of The Colony of New Haven*, the amateur historian was still the principal American historiographer. One gains the impression from his book that the only persons worthy of note are those of English descent and those whose ancestors settled in New England during the seventeenth century. While Lambert was dominated by a reverence for times past, and by accompanying genealogical associations, he did stress the importance of accurate history. Like Barber, he believed in placing in print fragments of local history that might otherwise be lost. Barber was complimentary about the past but was not a builder of written monuments to individuals. While Bacon also eulogized the early New England settlers, he did so in a way that rested more on the rudiments of historical research than on blind veneration. Because of Lambert's few footnotes one has to guess at the source of much of his information—which is also true of Barber and to a lesser degree of Bacon. Writing in the twentieth century Leonard W. Labaree had difficulty in uncovering some of Lambert's sources.[1] A close time and place similarity exists between Lambert, Bacon, and Barber. Lambert was not a theological interpreter of history, as was Bacon, nor did he have Barber's moral overtones. Viewpoints on slavery do not enter into Lambert's book—it was published before Cinque and the Amistad incident brought the issue more to the foreground. A reader may be impressed with the fact that Bacon is the more worldly of this group.

Atwater's *History of The Colony of New Haven* [1881] is a much more complete study than Lambert's or than comparable sections in the works of Bacon or Barber. It contains lengthy passages regarding everyday life in the early period of New Haven's settlement. His work on the city of New Haven [1887] revealed the trend in the late nineteenth century to undue glorification of localities had found a New Haven proponent. The city history is promotional in numerous ways, constantly praising New Haven in all its aspects, and containing many biographies and illustrations evidently paid for. In addition there are commercial advertisements within historical back-grounds. The city history includes many personal comments on New Haven daily life. Although Atwater could hardly be classified as a scholarly historian, he presents an increased scope and depth in comparison with earlier writers. While his indication of sources is slightly better than that of his predecessors, it is still deficient. The fact that Atwater was a clergyman is not reflected in his viewpoint, which, though a bit moral, is essentially factual. He does not dwell on genealogy as did Lambert, nor does he present an ecclesiastical interpretation of history as did Bacon, nor a righteous one as did Barber. Atwater's two books surveyed were published in the 1880s, the decade during which both Bacon and Barber died. Bacon, Barber, and then Atwater composed a group of writings both before and after the Civil War echoing anti-slavery viewpoints, although Atwater's post-war records tended only to confirm historical fact.

Levermore's *The Republic of New Haven* [1886] is a scholarly history. It explores in depth the evolution of New Haven's government and his statements were confirmed wherever possible by examination of original source material. Generally speaking Lambert, Bacon, Barber, and Atwater traced the history of New Haven to the early settlers and their English experience. Levermore suggests that the origins can be pursued to even earlier central European sources. While today this particular interpretation of historical roots is open to question, in its time it represented the result of current historical thought.[2] Levermore is objective and not influenced by sentiment, nor is his viewpoint affected by a worship of the past. His examination of the development of the governing process in New Haven leaves no stone unturned. Bacon's theological viewpoint and Barber's moral tendency contrast with Levermore's presentation, that of the academic researcher. He provided facts but left the major portion of interpretation to the reader, whereas the others rather liked to editorialize. Levermore satisfied the local need for a scholarly history, a need well in line with a national trend at the time he wrote. Like the works of Atwater, Levermore's study was published during the decade of Bacon's and Barber's death. Levermore had little time similarity with the latter two. While he had an evident feeling for New Haven, he did not possess the familiarity with the area of the other writers, nor did he have their intense sense of belonging. Consequently his writing is more detached. Levermore reveals an anti-slavery viewpoint, but, as in Atwater's case, he wrote after the Civil War. He is the concluding chapter in the progression of New Haven's nineteenth-century pattern of historical writing.

By the end of the century the history of New Haven was fairly well traced and recorded. Would New Haven's historiography have suffered appreciably without the writings of Bacon and Barber? It would have. While neither were born in New Haven, they were both New Haven in spirit and possessed strong emotional ties to the area and to its past. They wrote in the town-bred tradition and were particularly sentimental in their approach.

Leonard Bacon provides in his *Thirteen Historical Discourses* [1839] a religious history of New Haven from its beginnings up to and including the early nineteenth century. No similar history in such depth has been written. Oscar E. Maurer's *A Puritan Church* [1938] covers a greater span of time but in much less detail, and he depends on Bacon for a significant part of his material, though presenting some newly discovered information. *Thirteen Historical Discourses* is a major component of New Haven historiography. Had Bacon not written this book no one else would probably have contributed a similar study of comparable importance, for no other New Haven historical writer knew local church history so well. Bacon's other works add in a meaningful way to the general field of New Haven historiography. His *Slavery Discussed in Occasional Essays from 1833 to 1846* [1846] tells how New Haven's most prominent churchmen of the nineteenth century felt about the slavery issue. In his *Civil Government in The New Haven Colony* published in 1865 we are given a detailed examination of New Haven's early government. This article is a monument to the elaborate and thorough examination of a particular subject.

A list of some of Bacon's other works recalls the scope of his general contribution to local historical writing: *A Discourse on the Early Constitutional History of Connecticut*; *Sketch of the Life and Public Services of Hon. James Hillhouse of New Haven*; *New Haven, One Hundred Years Ago* and *Three Civic Orations for New Haven*. Bacon also wrote *Genesis of the New England Churches* which is both national and international in scope. He uniquely aided in preserving New Haven's history.

John Warner Barber published in 1831 his first edition of *History and Antiquities of New Haven*. A few years later Edward R. Lambert produced the *History of The Colony of New Haven* covering in many respects essentially the same ground. The fact indicates a demand at that time for historical works on the area. The question arises whether Barber's book awakened local interest to such a degree that it motivated Lambert to prepare his volume. Barber in *Connecticut Historical Collections* [1836] again provided historical information on New Haven but here gave it a broader background by studying the whole state as well. His record of events pertaining to the Amistad incident in *A History of the Amistad Captives* [1840] brings together much local material bearing on the case.

Barber's historical and geographical range is great, as mention of a few of his other books will indicate: *Interesting Events in the History of the United States*; *Massachusetts Historical Collections* and *The Loyal West in the Times of the Rebellion* (written in conjunction with Henry Howe). Barber was a pictorial illustrator. He was prolific, but reproduced in his New Haven historical works only what he himself had seen or what had been described to him. No survey of Barber's talents as a recorder of nineteenth century New Haven would be complete without an examination of his small volume entitled *Views in New Haven and its Vicinity* [1825]. Barber illustrated in a literal fashion. The depiction of local views was his greatest contribution. Barber's writings, even with the noted inaccuracies, are valuable in themselves, but when coupled with his illustrations he is seen as a truly significant local historian. New Haven of the times, and its surroundings, had no other recorder of its physical characteristics.

In Larned's *Literature of American History*, Bacon's *Genesis of the New England Churches* is the only book of Bacon's mentioned. Barber's *Connecticut Historical Collections* is listed, as well as a jointly written work dealing with another state. Also cited in Larned is Atwater's *History of The Colony of New Haven* and Levermore's *The Republic of New Haven.* Lambert is not listed.[3] The *Harvard Guide to American History* does not note writings by Bacon, Barber, or Lambert, but it does list Atwater's *History of The Colony of New Haven* as well as Levermore's *The Republic of New Haven.*[4] Bacon, Barber, and Levermore are included in the *Dictionary of American Biography*, but not Lambert or Atwater.

Bacon occasionally used the memories of older persons. Barber was an extensive recorder of the recollections of those he interviewed. Barber felt it was his duty to record everything of an historical nature as it came to his attention, as well as to preserve source material through quotations. Lambert proceeded in somewhat the same manner. It should be remembered, of course, that at the time there was a scarcity of centers where published historical works or original source materials could be examined.

Bacon included in his works many intricate details of New Haven's early history, events usually with a direct or indirect ecclesiastical connection. Bacon's evident devotion to his own church and to religion in general give his writings the overtone of a church history. Many of his published works resulted from reworking sermons or addresses. An example is *Funeral Discourse, Pronounced at the Interment of the Hon. James Hillhouse.* Similar in approach is *A Discourse on the Traffic in Spirituous Liquors, with an Appendix Exhibiting the Present State and Influence of the Traffic in The City of New Haven.* In several writings outside the sphere of New Haven history Barber displayed a preoccupation with religious matters, embracing an extremely moral viewpoint. These works include *Historical Religious Events, The Bible Looking Glass*, and *The Picture Preacher*. Here Barber provided for the individual lay reader or family group a presentation of religious history and teachings. He stressed religion's relevance to everyday life. Barber, without church or pulpit, used his writings to project his thoughts.

Bacon had an orderly approach in his writing. This is illustrated by the logical and chronological presentation of material in *Thirteen Historical Discourses*. His footnotes are more complete than Barber's and his investigations were made in greater depth. Barber was haphazard, as seen in the disorganized structure of *History and Antiquities of New Haven* and in the New Haven section of *Connecticut Historical Collections*. This would lead one to believe that Bacon was generally more accurate and thorough than Barber.

American historiography of the early and mid-nineteenth century features expression of local pride, an interest in everyday customs of the past, and a respect for ancestors coupled with representations of their virtues. Generally there was little use of original source materials. During this time there were traces of romantic nationalism along with the theme of continuing betterment. The documentary history was a significant factor. Such a description would also define the historical writings of both Bacon and Barber.

The various histories of an urban area aid a city in forming a consciousness of its own existence.[5] All of the five historians surveyed so contributed to New Haven—Leonard Bacon and John Warner Barber to a greater degree than the others. Bacon and Barber have some of the characteristics of the over-praising historian of the late nineteenth century but as scholarly historians they were essentially of a different and earlier school. Our debt to both Leonard Bacon and John Warner Barber is greater than a merely cursory examination of their works would indicate. While their contribution to New Haven history is often lightly treated or overlooked, the passage of time should not dim but only enhance the significance of their work.

Yale College *circa* 1830. Drawing and engraving attributed to J. W. Barber

Epilogue

Two significant scholarly works written since 1930 have succeeded and connected the New Haven histories which appeared in the nineteenth century. They are Isabel MacBeath Calder's *The New Haven Colony* [1934] and a work of much greater scope, Rollin G. Osterweis's *Three Centuries of New Haven, 1638-1938* [1953].

In her preface Calder wrote that the previous histories of the Colony, by Lambert, Atwater, and Levermore, left a great deal of ground uncovered, especially in overlooking original manuscripts. She naturally questioned the accuracy of these earlier writers. In the preface Calder makes no reference to either Bacon or Barber and the bibliographical note also excludes Barber.[1] She cites Bacon's *Thirteen Historical Discourses* three times, and Atwater's *History of The Colony of New Haven* five times, including its references to its maps of early New Haven and Milford homelots. Lambert's *History of The Colony of New Haven* is cited four times but essentially only to correct the earlier work. *The Republic of New Haven* by Levermore does not appear in the footnotes although it is mentioned in the bibliographical note.

Throughout Calder's *The New Haven Colony* the depth of research is evident. Her investigations support the historical interpretation that the Puritans were close to Anglicans on questions of faith while far apart on those of church organization and government. She interjects a bit of realism with the following statement:

> " . . . after the lapse of three hundred years it is possible to see the humor in the excommunication of the first lady of the colony [Mrs. Theophilus Eaton], who knew the walled city of Chester and its cathedral, from the £ 500 church in the center of seventeenth-century New Haven by those who had crossed the Atlantic to avoid religious persecution."[2]

In this same vein, the reason for the New Haven Colony's greater propensity to trade with Quakers than that of her sister members of the United Colonies of New England is in order to " . . . lose no penny of profit which might accrue to the merchants. . . . " Continuing in a somewhat humorous tone Calder states that the investigators sent by Charles II to New England in 1664 came to the conclusion that Indians listened to Puritan sermons because they were paid to do so. She clearly states her position on the absorption of the New Haven Colony into Connecticut.

> The grant [Royal Charter] to Connecticut was probably made without thought of the consequences to the New Haven Colony. There is not a scrap of evidence that the king intended to abolish the colony on the Sound to

punish it for sheltering Edward Whalley and William Goffe, the regicides.[3]

Calder's work is excellent scholarship but deals only with a short and early period of New Haven's history. Her services are a superior guide to further detailed research on the Colony.

Rollin G. Osterweis's *Three Centuries of New Haven, 1638-1938* [1953] encompasses the entire spectrum of New Haven history up to 1938. This work is in the nature of an official Tercentenary History. It was commissioned in 1947 by The New Haven Colony Historical Society (using funds made available through the New Haven Tercentenary Committee). The Society requested that the history be of interest to the general reader and also of value to the scholar.[4] Both criteria are fulfilled.

Osterweis begins by reminding the reader that New Haven's early settlers were deeply religious. They "identified their trials and aspirations with those of the children of Israel." But the settlement had a dual character: "Both religious and economic motives brought the founders of New Haven to Connecticut."[5]

Osterweis mentions that the fairness of New Haven's early settlers to the Quinnipiack Indians was in favourable contrast to the general treatment granted Indians elsewhere. Early New Haveners never considered they were establishing a democracy but thought in terms of a Bible Commonwealth. There is an emphasis on the town: " . . . we must not forget that the town preceded the colony, dominated the colony, and survived the colony."[6]

There were Negroes, probably slaves, at New Haven as early as 1646. Referring to the Amistad affair, Osterweis comments on the humanitarian aspects of New Haven's response: " . . . it led the opinion of that city [New Haven] to follow the path of humanitarianism rather than that of economic self-interest or of apathetic indifference [concerning slavery]." The text includes a specific summary of the overall experience of New Haven's

Negro population during the period from the late eighteenth century to the Civil War.[7] Osterweis points out that at the head of the list of possible crimes against the Colony was an attempt to overthrow the state. In a religious commonwealth such action would be far more than a political offense since it implied an attack upon God and His elect.[8] His views on the passing of the Colony are similar to those of Calder's.

> The present writer is inclined for the most part to stand with the interpretation of Professor Andrews, that the hiding of the "the Colonels" [Regicides] did not cause the fall of the jurisdiction. Yet the episode may well have angered Charles II sufficiently to encourage his ignoring of New Haven in the issuance of the Charter of 1662 [to Connecticut].[9]

Osterweis includes much social history. He comments that late seventeenth-century New Haven was a somewhat sleepy town where insignificant matters took on major proportions. The term "poor seaport town" is also used. In the mid-eighteenth century New Haven began to emerge from its medieval period. "The English colonial village of 1665 had slowly evolved through eleven decades into a cosmopolitan, self-assured American community."[10]

New Haven architecture receives its due recognition throughout the book. The reader's attention is called to the three early nineteenth-century churches still standing on the Green, two with Greek Revival features, Center and United, and Trinity with its Gothic Revival appearance. These were products of the Romantic movement in America, as was also the Egyptian-style gateway of the Grove Street Cemetery. The Green offers a thread of continuity to New Haven in the midst of change. A description of New Haven in 1900 continues the author's architectural observations: "A city of brownstone, limestone, brick and iron had sprung up in the nine original squares—a city of Victorian architecture."[11]

Osterweis, commenting that the American Revolution was no less a civil conflict than the Civil War, observes that life in New Haven immediately after the Revolution experienced few radical departures from the past.[12] (Yale was the largest colonial college before the Revolution and remained so after peace had come.)[13] The transition from town to city government during the late eighteenth century is documented, but Osterweis notes that the characteristics of a small colonial town remained. The beginnings of an industrial New Haven in the period after the Revolution are reviewed. The contribution of Eli Whitney—whose cotton gin fastened a cotton and slave economy on the South—to local industry with the opening of his gun factory in Hamden in 1798 is mentioned. Throughout the book we are reminded of harbor and waterfront activity. Of interest are the references to New Haven's South Sea's fleet of about 1800 and to Long Wharf.[14]

Osterweis presents James Hillhouse as the late eighteenth- and early nineteenth-century personification of New Haven's civic consciousness. In the pre-Civil War period James Brewster was known as the grand old man of New Haven industry. Brewster's carriage factory symbolized the business achievements of the City. The later contributions to New Haven's business leadership by representatives of recent immigration are also reported. Nineteenth-century immigration to New Haven is explored in detail, and Osterweis mentions that the area's accessibility to the port of New York made it the chief receiving point for Connecticut immigrants bringing waves of Irish, Germans, Italians, and others to the City. And finally in New Haven " . . . the Italian immigrant gave way to the Italian-American, who was in turn superseded by the American of Italian ancestry."[15] New Haven's emergence as a modern city is thoroughly reported. We are led into the twentieth century. "One gets a sense of mushrooming growth from it all, with the accompanying thought that the old emphasis upon planning and beauty had been submerged."[16]

A summation of the drive for civic improvement after the turn of the century, an examination of the effect on New Haven of the First World War, and a description of the gay twenties and sober thirties bring us to the time of the Tercentenary.[17] Osterweis remarks that the anniversaries of both Connecticut in 1936 and New Haven in 1938 led to an outpouring of local pride which resulted in an appraisal of modern achievements as well as a remembrance of the past. The major New Haven themes of religion and education, persisting throughout its history, along with economic advancement jointed to civic improvement, survived to the Tercentenary year.[18]

Notes

A Survey

1. Michael Kraus, *A History of American History* (New York: Farrar and Rinehart, 1937), pp. 176-179.

2. David D. Van Tassel, *Recording America's Past: An Interpretation of the Development of Historical Studies in America: 1607-1884* (Chicago: The University of Chicago Press, 1960), pp. 51-92, passim.

3. Kraus, op. cit., pp. 183-185.

4. Van Tassel, op. cit., p. 93.

5. John Warner Barber, *Interesting Events in the History of the United States* (New Haven: J. W. Barber, 1828), p. iv.

6. Van Tassel, op. cit., pp. 109-110.

7. Oscar Handlin and others, *Harvard Guide to American History* (Cambridge, Massachusetts: The Belknap Press of Harvard University Press, 1954), p. 4.

8. Kraus, op. cit., pp. 200-238, passim.

9. Handlin, op. cit., pp. 4-5.

10. Kraus, op. cit., pp. 181-183.

11. W. Stull Holt, *Historical Scholarship in the United States and other Essays*, Part I, Historical Scholarship and the Historical Profession (Seattle: University of Washington Press, 1967), p. 47.

12. Van Tassel, op. cit., pp. 111-113.

13. Kraus, op. cit., pp. 272-273.

14. Handlin, op. cit., p. 7.

15. Ibid., p. 57.

16. Van Tassel, op. cit., pp. 122-124..

17. Ibid., pp. 94-159, passim.

18. Handlin, op. cit., p. 5.

19. Van Tassel, op. cit., pp. 161-177, passim.

20. Handlin, op. cit., p. 5.

21. Kraus, op. cit., pp. 321-333, passim.

22. Holt, op. cit., pp. 3-26, passim.

23. Handlin, op. cit., p. 6.

24. Van Tassel, op. cit., p. viii.

25. Daniel Horowitz, "The Meaning of City Biographies: New Haven in the Nineteenth and Early Twentieth Centuries," *The Connecticut Historical Society Bulletin*, Volume 29, No. 3 (July, 1964), p. 66.

26. Holt, op. cit., pp. 32-63, passim.

27. Handlin, op. cit., p. 13.

28. Walter Muir Whitehill, *Independent Historical Societies* (Boston: The Boston Athenaeum, 1962), p. 349.

29. Ibid., p. x, and also Leslie W. Dunlap, *American Historical Societies, 1790-1860* (Madison, Wisconsin: Privately Printed, 1944), p. vii.

30. Elizabeth Linscott, "Early Years of Our First Historical Society," *The New England Galaxy*, IX (Winter, 1968), 18-21.

31. Van Tassel, op. cit., pp. 61-62.

32. Handlin, op. cit., p. 13.

33. Van Tassel, op. cit., pp. 59-109, passim.

34. Whitehill, op. cit., p. 88.

35. The New Haven Colony Historical Society, *The English Memorial* (New Haven: The New Haven Colony Historical Society, 1893), pp. 62-71, *passim.* and also Yale University, *The Buildings of Yale University* (Bulletin of Yale University, Series 61, No. 3. New Haven: Yale University, 1965), p. 90.

36. Van Tassel, op. cit., p. 175. and also Handlin, op. cit., p. 14.

37. Van Tassel, op. cit., pp. 65-66.

38. Whitehill, op. cit., p. 427.

Leonard Bacon

1. Leonard Bacon, *Thirteen Historical Discourses, on the Completion of Two Hundred Years, from the Beginning of The First Church in New Haven* (New Haven: Durrie and Peck, 1839), pp. iii-vi.

2. Ibid., pp. 2-15, passim.

3. Ibid., pp. 17-36, passim.

4. Ibid., pp. 43-53, passim.

5. Ibid., pp. 53-73, passim.

6. Ibid., p. 75.

7. Ibid., p. 83.

8. Ibid., pp. 85-86.

9. Ibid., pp. 91-94.

10. Ibid., p. 94.

11. Ibid., pp. 95-96.

12. Ibid., pp. 117-154, passim.

13. Ibid., pp. 160-162.

14. Ibid., pp. 167, 168.

15. Ibid., p. 170.

16. Ibid., pp. 183-192.

17. Ibid., p. 193.

18. Ibid., pp. 209, 210.

19. Ibid., p. 211.

20. Ibid., p. 223.

21. Ibid., p. 239.

22. Ibid., pp. 241-242.

23. Ibid., p. 248.

24. Ibid., pp. 255-266, passim.

25. Ibid., p. 267.

26. Ibid., p. 275.

27. Ibid., pp. 277, 278.

28. Ibid., pp. 280-281, 284, 285.

29. Ibid., p. 286.

30. Ibid., p. 288.

31. Leonard Bacon. *Slavery Discussed in Occasional Essays from 1833 to 1846* (New York: Baker and Scribner, 1846), p. iii.

32. Ibid., pp. viii-x.

33. Ibid., pp. 14-24, passim.

34. Ibid., pp. 24-47, passim.

35. Ibid., pp. 50-56, passim.

36. Ibid., pp. 57-68, passim.

37. Ibid., pp. 85-105, passim.

38. Ibid., pp. 114-121, passim.

39. Ibid., p. 125.

40. Ibid., pp. 142-143, 170.

41. Ibid., pp. 180-200, passim, p. 203.

42. Ibid., p. 208.

43. Ibid., pp. 220-224, passim, p. 246.

44. Leonard Bacon, "Civil Government in The New Haven Colony," *Papers of The New Haven Colony Historical Society*, Vol. I (New Haven, 1865), p. 11.

45. Ibid., pp. 12-13. Isabel Calder in *The New Haven Colony*, p. 51, contends that the day of extraordinary humiliation was at New Haven

while Rollin G. Osterweis in *Three Centuries of New Haven, 1638-1938*, pp. 14-15, supports Bacon's position.

46. Bacon, "Civil Government," op. cit., p. 14.

47. Ibid., pp. 13-23, passim, p. 15.

48. Ibid., p. 16.

John Warner Barber

1. The Amistad incident is described in the biography of Leonard Bacon, *supra* p. 11

2. John Warner Barber, *History and Antiquities of New Haven* (Conn.) *from its Earliest Settlement to the Present Time* (New Haven: J. W. Barber, 1831/1832), pp. 3-12, passim.

3. Ibid., p. 13.

4. Ibid., pp. 16-18, 30-33, 63-77, 83-100, passim.

5. Ibid., pp. 20, 62, 82, 111.

6. Ibid., p. 24.

7. Ibid., p. 29.

8. Ibid., pp. 82-83.

9. Ibid., pp. 107-108.

10. Ibid., pp. 118-120.

11. John Warner Barber, *Connecticut Historical Collections* (second edition; New Haven; Durrie and Peck and J. W. Barber, 1836), p. iii.

12. Ibid., pp. iii-iv.

13. Ibid., p. iv.

14. Ibid., p. 149.

15. Ibid., p. iv.

16. Ibid., pp. 13-16, 161, 285-288, 389.

17. Ibid., p. 17.

18. Ibid., pp. 101, 133, 194, 219.

19. Ibid., pp. 133, 159.

20. Ibid., p. 504.

21. Ibid., pp. 238, 358, 487, 543, 549, 560.

22. Ibid., pp. 134, 135, 137.

23. Ibid., p. 135: Bacon, "Civil Government in The New Haven Colony," pp. 12-14.

24. Barber, C. H. C., op. cit., pp. 154-155; Franklin B. Dexter, "Memoranda Respecting Edward Whalley and William Goffe," *Papers of The New Haven Colony Historical Society*, Vol. II. (New Haven: The New Haven Colony Historical Society, 1877), passim.

25. Barber, C. H. C., op. cit., pp. 159-163, 184-185.

26. Ibid., pp. 173, 200, 265, 309, 391, 426, 429, 489, 492, 238.

27. Ibid., pp. 196, 230; Rollin G. Osterweis, *Three Centuries of New Haven, 1638-1938* (New Haven: Yale University Press, 1953), p. 30.

28. Barber, C. H. C., op. cit., p. 199.

29. Ibid., pp. 232, 264.

30. Ibid., pp. 556-557.

31. Ibid., p. 489.

32. John W. Barber (comp.), *A History of the Amistad Captives* (New Haven: E. L. and J. W. Barber, 1840), preface.

33. Ibid., pp. 5-15, passim.

34. Ibid., pp. 9, 21-23.

35. Ibid., pp. 24-25.

36. Ibid., pp. 25-28.

37. Ibid., pp. 29-31.

Edward Rodolphus Lambert

1. Edward R. Lambert, *History of The Colony of New Haven* (New Haven: Hitchcock and Stafford, 1838), pp. 3, 13.

2. Ibid., pp. 3-4, 41, 52.

3. Ibid., p. 20.

4. Ibid., p. 61., Franklin B. Dexter, "Memoranda Respecting Edward Whalley and William Goffe," *Papers of The New Haven Colony Historical Society*, Vol. II (New Haven: The New Haven Colony Historical Society, 1877), passim.

5. Lambert, op. cit., pp. 80-81.

6. Ibid., p. 204.

7. Ibid., pp. 205, 216.

Edward Elias Atwater

1. Edward E. Atwater, *History of The Colony of New Haven* (New Haven: Privately Printed, 1881), pp. iii-iv.

2. Ibid., pp. v, 73.

3. Ibid., pp. 2-3.

4. Ibid., p. 80.

5. Ibid., pp. 188, 215-216, 226-227, 260.

6. Ibid., pp. 325, 359, 365, 372.

7. Ibid., pp. 419-420, 528.

8. Edward E. Atwater (ed.), *History of The City of New Haven* (New York: W. W. Munsell and Company, 1887), p. iii.

9. Ibid., p. 10.

10. Ibid., p. 54.

11. Ibid., p. 65.

12. Ibid., p. 69.

13. Ibid., p. 162.

14. Ibid., p. 205.

15. Ibid., p. 213.

16. Ibid., p. 338.

17. Ibid., pp. 351, 379, 409-410, 416

Charles Herbert Levermore

1. Charles H. Levermore, *The Republic of New Haven* (Baltimore: Johns Hopkins University, 1886), preface.

2. Ibid., pp. 50-51, 86.

3. Ibid., pp. 32, 154, 178.

4. Ibid., pp. 70-74, 132-134.

5. Ibid., p. 202.

6. Ibid., pp. 203, 228-230.

7. Ibid., pp. 252-254.

8. Ibid., p. 257.

9. Ibid., p. 280.

10. Ibid., p. 285.

Summary of New Haven Nineteenth-Century Historiography

1. Leonard W. Labaree, *Milford, Connecticut: The Early Development of a Town as Shown in its Land Records* (New Haven: Tercentenary Commission of the State of Connecticut, 1933,) p. 30.

2. Isabel MacBeath Calder, *The New Haven Colony* (New Haven: Yale University Press, 1934), p. v. (reprinted 1970, Archon Books)

3. J. N. Larned (ed.), *The Literature of American History: A Bibliographical Guide* (Boston: Houghton Mifflin and Company, 1902), passim.

4. Oscar Handlin and others, *Harvard Guide to American History* (Cambridge, Massachusetts: The Belknap Press of Harvard University Press, 1954), pp. 221, 270.

5. Daniel Horowitz, "The Meaning of City Biographies: New Haven in the Nineteenth and Early Twentieth Centuries," p. 65.

Epilogue

1. Isabel MacBeath Calder, *The New Haven Colony*, pp. v, 271-2.

2. Ibid., p. 93.

3. Ibid., pp. 97, 177, 230. For information supporting the contrary interpretation see Atwater, *History of The Colony of New Haven*, pp. 438-443, and *History of The City of New Haven*, p. 7; Charles H. Levermore, *The Republic of New Haven*, pp. 111-113. Rollin G. Osterweis in *Three Centuries of New Haven, 1638-1938*, pp. 63-64 summarizes conflicting viewpoints while generally supporting Calder's interpretation.

4. Rollin G. Osterweis, *Three Centuries of New Haven, 1638-1938*, p. vii.

5. Ibid., pp. 3, 6.

6. Ibid., pp. 11, 14, 32.

7. Ibid., pp. 33, 287-290, 297.

8. Ibid., p. 41.

9. Ibid., pp. 63-64.

10. Ibid., pp. 72, 74, 76, 112-113.

11. Ibid., pp. 204-205, 210, 264, 387.

12. Ibid., p. 127, 151.

13. Ibid., p. 152.

14. Ibid., pp. 162, 172, 183, 186, 193, 201, 206, 244, 330, 386, 427.

15. Ibid., pp. 254-255, 262, 282, 318, 372.

16. Ibid., p. 388.

17. Ibid., pp. 390-424, passim.

18. Ibid., pp. 423-424, 427.

Bibliography

Abbott, Morris W. "Notes on the Life of Edward Rodolphus Lambert," Milford, Connecticut: 1970. (Xeroxed copy may be examined at The New Haven Colony Historical Society)

Adams, Henry. *History of the United States*. 9 vols. New York: Charles Scribner's Sons, 1889-91.

Andrews, Charles M. *The Colonial Period of American History: The Settlements*. Vol. II. New Haven: Yale University Press, 1936.

Atwater, Edward E. *History of The Colony of New Haven to its Absorption into Connecticut*. New Haven: Privately Printed, 1881.

"Atwater, Edward E." *Historical and Biographical Record of the Class of 1836, in Yale College, for Fifty Years from the Admission of the Class to College.* New Haven: L. S. Punderson, Printer, 1882. Pp. 25-26.

"Atwater." *Historical and Biographical Record of the Class of 1836, in Yale College. An Appendix, Containing Minutes of the Class Meeting at Commencement, June, 1886.* P. 5.

Atwater, Edward E. (ed.). *History of The City of New Haven.* New York: W. W. Munsell and Company, 1887.

"Atwater, Elias Edward." *Obituary Record of Graduates of Yale University, Deceased from June, 1880, to June, 1890,* New Haven: Tuttle, Morehouse and Taylor, Printers, 1890. Pp. 434-435.

Bacon, Leonard. *Funeral Discourse, Pronounced at the Interment of the Hon. James Hillhouse, January 2, 1833.* New Haven: Baldwin and Ellis, 1833.

_____. *A Discourse on the Traffic in Spirituous Liquors, with an Appendix Exhibiting the Present State and Influence of the Traffic in The City of New Haven.* New Haven: B. L. Hamlen, 1838.

_____. *Thirteen Historical Discourses, on the Completion of Two Hundred Years, from the Beginning of The First Church in New Haven.* New Haven: Durrie and Peck, 1839.

_____. *A Discourse on the Early Constitutional History of Connecticut.* Hartford: Case, Tiffany and Burnham, 1843.

_____. *Slavery Discussed in Occasional Essays from 1833 to 1846.* New York: Baker and Scribner, 1846.

_____. *Sketch of the Life and Public Services of Hon. James Hillhouse of New Haven.* New Haven: Privately Printed, 1860.

_____. "Civil Government in The New Haven Colony," *Papers of The New Haven Colony Historical Society.* Vol. I. New Haven: The New Haven Colony Historical Society, 1865. Pp. 11-27.

_____. *Genesis of the New England Churches.* New York: Harper, 1874.

_____.*New Haven: One Hundred Years Ago.* New Haven: F. P. Shanley, 1876.

_____. *Three Civic Orations for New Haven.* New Haven: Tuttle, Morehouse and Taylor, 1879.

Leonard Bacon: Pastor of The First Church in New Haven. New Haven: Tuttle, Morehouse and Taylor, 1882.

Bancroft, George. *History of the United States from the Discovery of the American Continent.* 10 vols. Boston: Little, Brown and Company, 1834-74.

Barber, J. W. *Views in New Haven and its Vicinity.* New Haven: J. W. Barber and A. H. Maltby and Company. 1825.

Barber, John W. *Historical Scenes in the United States.* New Haven: Monson and Company, 1827.

_____. *Historical Religious Events: Being a Selection of the Most Important and Interesting Religious Events which have Transpired Since the Commencement of the Christian Era to the Present Time.* Hartford: D. F. Robinson and Company, 1828.

Barber, John Warner. *Interesting Events in the History of the United States.* New Haven: J. W. Barber, 1828.

_____. *History and Antiquities of New Haven, (Conn.) from its Earliest Settlement to the Present Time.* New Haven: J. W. Barber, 1831. Second edition. 1831/1832. Third edition. 1831/1846. Fourth edition. John W. Barber and Lemuel S. Punderson, 1856. Fifth edition. John W. Barber and Lemuel S. Punderson, 1870.

_____. *Connecticut Historical Collections.* Second edition. New Haven: Durrie and Peck and J. W. Barber, 1836.

Barber, John W. *Massachusetts Historical Collections.* Worcester: Dorr, Howland and Company, 1839.

_____. (comp.). *A History of the Amistad Captives.* New Haven: E. L. and J. W. Barber, 1840.

Barber, John W. and Elizabeth G. Barber. *Historical, Poetical and Pictorial American Scenes.* New Haven: J. W. Barber for J. W. Bradley, 1850.

Barber, John W. *European Historical Collections: Comprising England, Scotland, with Holland, Belgium and Part of France.* New Haven: John W. Barber, 1855.

Barber, John Warner, and Henry Howe. *The Loyal West in the Times of the Rebellion.* Cincinnati: F. A. Howe, 1865.

Barber, John W., and others. *The Bible Looking Glass.* Philadelphia: Bradley, Garretson and Company, 1878.

Barber, John Warner. *The Picture Preacher: A Book of Morals.* New Haven: Henry Howe, 1880.

Bartlett, Ellen Strong. *A New Haven Church.* New Haven: The First Church of Christ in New Haven, 1954.

Bingham, Hiram. *Elihu Yale.* New York: Dodd, Mead and Company, 1939. (Reprinted 1968, Archon Books)

Calder, Isabel MacBeath. *The New Haven Colony.* New Haven: Yale University Press, 1934. (Reprinted 1970, Archon Books)

Dexter, Franklin B. "Memoranda Respecting Edward Whalley and William Goffe," *Papers of The New Haven Colony Historical Society.* Vol. II. New Haven: The New Haven Colony Historical Society, 1877. Pp. 117-146.

Dexter, Franklin Bowditch. *Sketch of the History of Yale University.* New York: Henry Holt and Company, 1887.

Dinsmore, Charles Allen. "Leonard Bacon," *Dictionary of American Biography*, Vol. I. New York: Charles Scribner's Sons, 1928. Pp. 479-481.

Dondore, Dorothy Anne. "Henry Howe," *Dictionary of American Biography*, Vol. V. New York: Charles Scribner's Sons, 1928. Pp. 288-289.

Dunlap, Leslie W. *American Historical Societies, 1790-1860.* Madison, Wisconsin: Privately Printed, 1944.

Goodrich, Laurence B. *Ralph Earl: Recorder for an Era.* The State University of New York, 1967.

Handlin, Oscar, and others. *Harvard Guide to American History.* Cambridge, Massachusetts: The Belknap Press of Harvard University Press, 1954.

Hockett, Homer Carey. *The Critical Method in Historical Research and Writing*. New York: The Macmillan Company, 1955.

Holmes, Abiel. *American Annals*. 2 vols. Cambridge, Massachusetts: W. Hilliard, 1805.

Holmes, John Haynes. "Charles Herbert Levermore," *Dictionary of American Biography*, Vol. XI. New York: Charles Scribner's Sons, 1933. Pp. 199-200.

Holt, W. Stull. *Historical Scholarship in the United States and other Essays*. Part I, Historical Scholarship and the Historical Profession. Seattle: University of Washington Press, 1967.

Horowitz, Daniel. "The Meaning of City Biographies: New Haven in the Nineteenth and Early Twentieth Centuries," *The Connecticut Historical Society Bulletin*. Vol. 29. No. 3. Hartford: The Connecticut Historical Society, 1964. Pp. 65-75.

Hotchkiss, Herbert A. "Editorial." *The Connecticut Nutmegger*, September, 1970, p. 121.

Howe, Henry. *Historical Collections of Virginia*. Charleston, South Carolina: Babcock and Company, 1845.

Kraus, Michael. *A History of American History*. New York: Farrar and Rinehart, 1937.

Labaree, Leonard W. *Milford, Connecticut: The Early Development of a Town as Shown in its Land Records*. New Haven: Tercentenary Commission of the State of Connecticut, 1933.

Lambert, Edward R. *History of The Colony of New Haven, Before and After the Union with Connecticut*. New Haven: Hitchcock and Stafford, 1838.

Larned, J. N. (ed.). *The Literature of American History: A Bibliographical Guide*. Boston: Houghton Mifflin and Company, 1902.

Levermore, Charles H. *The Republic of New Haven: A History of Municipal Evolution*. Baltimore: Johns Hopkins University, 1886.

"Levermore, Charles Herbert." *Obituary Record of Graduates Deceased During the Year Ending July 1, 1928. No. 87.* New Haven: Yale University, 1928. Pp. 73-75.

Linscott, Elizabeth. "Early Years of Our First Historical Society." *The New England Galaxy*, IX (Winter, 1968), 18-24.

Mahan, Alfred Thayer. *The Influence of Sea Power upon History.* Third edition. Boston: Little, Brown and Company, 1893.

Mather, Cotton. *Magnalia Christi Americana.* 7 vols. in 1. London: Thomas Parkhurst, 1702.

Maurer, Oscar E. *A Puritan Church.* New Haven: Yale University Press, 1938.

Nash, Chauncey Cushing. *John Warner Barber and His Books.* Milton, Massachusetts: Reprinted from the Note Book of the Walpole Society, 1934.

Vital Records of New Haven 1649-1850. 2 vols. Hartford, Connecticut: The Connecticut Society of the Order of the Founders and Patriots of America, 1917-1924.

Papers of The New Haven Colony Historical Society. Vol. III. New Haven: The New Haven Colony Historical Society, 1882.

The New Haven Colony Historical Society. *The English Memorial.* New Haven: The New Haven Colony Historical Society, 1893.

Olney, J., and John W. Barber. *The Family Book of History.* New Haven: Durrie and Peck, 1839.

Osterweis, Rollin G. *Three Centuries of New Haven, 1638-1938.* New Haven: Yale University Press, 1953.

Parkman, Francis. *The Parkman Reader.* Edited by Samuel Eliot Morison. Boston: Little, Brown and Company, 1955.

Smith, Ralph C. "John Warner Barber," *Dictionary of American Biography*, Vol. I. New York: Charles Scribner's Sons, 1928. P. 589.

Sparks, Jared. *The Life of George Washington.* Boston: F. Andrews, 1839.

Townshend, Henry H. "John W. Barber, Illustrator and Historian," *Papers of The New Haven Colony Historical Society.* Vol. X. New Haven: The New Haven Colony Historical Society, 1951. Pp. 313-336.

Trumbull, Benjamin. *A Complete History of Connecticut, Civil and Ecclesiastical, to 1764.* 2 vols. New Haven: Maltby, Goldsmith and Company and Samuel Wadsworth, 1818.

Turner, Frederick Jackson. *The Frontier in American History.* New York: H. Holt and Company, 1920.

Van Dusen, Albert E. *Connecticut.* New York: Random House, 1961.

Van Tassel, David D. *Recording America's Past: An Interpretation of the Development of Historical Studies in America: 1607-1884.* Chicago: The University of Chicago Press, 1960.

Whitehill, Walter Muir. *Independent Historical Societies.* Boston: The Boston Athenaeum, 1962.

Williams, F. W. "Charles Herbert Levermore," *A History of the Class of Seventy-Nine, Yale College, During the Thirty Years from its Admission into the Academic Department, 1875-1905.* Cambridge: The University Press, 1906. Pp. 266-270.

Winsor, Justin (ed.). *Narrative and Critical History of America.* 8 vols. Boston: Houghton Mifflin Company, 1884-89.

Yale University. *The Buildings of Yale University.* Bulletin of Yale University, Series 61, No. 3. New Haven: Yale University, 1965.